Enter
Into
AIKIDO

Dear Carol,

I am glad to have you as a Qigang student. I hope this book helps you on your journey,

Soku-dai

Enter
Into
AIKIDO

DAVID NEMEROFF

TATE PUBLISHING & Enterprises

This book is designed to provide accurate and authoritative information with regard to the subject matter covered. This information is given with the understanding that neither the author nor Tate Publishing, LLC is engaged in rendering legal, professional advice. Since the details of your situation are fact dependent, you should additionally seek the services of a competent professional.

The opinions expressed by the author are not necessarily those of Tate Publishing, LLC.

Published by Tate Publishing & Enterprises, LLC
127 E. Trade Center Terrace | Mustang, Oklahoma 73064 USA
1.888.361.9473 | www.tatepublishing.com

Tate Publishing is committed to excellence in the publishing industry.

Book design copyright © 2009 by Tate Publishing, LLC. All rights reserved.
Cover design by Chris Castor
Interior design by Lindsay B. Behrens
Photos taken by Christopher Allen

Published in the United States of America

ISBN: 978-1-60799-272-1
1. Sports and Recreation   2. Martial Arts/Aikido
09.03.30

Dedication

I want to dedicate this book to my loving wife, Adria, who is my light. Her constant support and unconditional love have meant so much to me. She is integral to my life. Thank you, Adria. I love you.

Acknowledgments

I could not have written this book without the teachings of Cary Nemeroff, Soke; Dr. Jose Andrade, Sensei; and Sifu Bernard Seif. Thank you, Soke, for taking my training to places I never thought I could go. You have been a great inspiration to me as well as being an integral part of making martial arts a permanent fixture in my life. Andrade, Sensei, thank you for your never–ending generosity and guidance. You have taught me not only about martial arts technique, but a way to live in harmony. I will always remember that "Life should be a vacation." You are a mentor, a great teacher, and a friend. Robert MacEwen Jr., Sensei, thank you for introducing me to such a wonderful art and motivating me to explore it further. Sifu Bernard Seif, I appreciate your kindness and open heart. All of their teachings and insight have helped me to evolve into who I am today. I also give my gratitude to Shizuya Sato and the other sensei of Kokusai Budoin, for all of your instruction and allowing me to be a part of such a wonderful organization. Further thanks to Cary Nemeroff, Soke, Jose Andrade, Sensei and Paul Godshaw, Shihan for your kind words about me and this book.

I also appreciate the support and feedback of all my friends, including Christopher Allen, Amy Edel–Vaugn, Mark Wawrzenski, and Jason Neff who helped me greatly with this book by listening to my ideas and challenging my thoughts. Dr. Kenneth Choquette, thank you for your medical insight, your helpful information, and your friendship. Thank you, Christopher Allen, for taking the photos for this book. Also, a special appreciation to the following students who contributed to this text: David George, Sensei, Nicolas Fulton, Sensei, Dodie Sable, Sensei, Benjamin Staples, Wade Bailey, Jeremiah Henning, Christopher Myers, Joshua Dasilva, Jeremy Dasilva, Justin Johannsmeier, Thomas Titano, Alex Tejera, Jason Pagan, Elbis Medina, Ashley St. Louis, Bradley St. Louis, Mallory Zingone, and Richard Setyanto.

I also want to give my appreciation to my caring parents, Susan and Bernard, and my beautiful wife, Adria, for always being there. Finally, a thanks to my students and the other sensei who preserve the integrity of traditional martial arts, the pursuit of self–exploration and the discovery of one's true self.

Table of Contents

Foreword

Enter into Aikido, by David Nemeroff, is a must for an aspiring student of the martial arts, parents searching for a dojo or martial arts class for their kids, the student of aikido, and any dojo library. It uniquely draws upon the aikido and general martial arts experience of the author and includes testimonials by others who share their perceptions about what they experienced while training in a traditional martial arts dojo.

This innovative guide gives the novice or prospective student a clear idea about what to expect of a martial arts dojo and, furthermore, can help one to make an educated decision about where they'd most enjoy training. For the advanced aikido or general martial arts practitioner, this is a great reference manual that answers questions to just about anything dealing with the Asian martial arts.

David Nemeroff, Master of Fukasa–Ryu Aikido, has been training regularly as a student of mine for over two decades. His career is dedicated to teaching the martial arts, and he continues to supplement his training in aikido with Fukasa–Ryu Aiki–Bujutsu, the original Samurai arts from which aikido evolved. I am proud to have him as my most senior student… He is currently the director of the Fukasa–Ryu Aikido Division of Fukasa–Kai.

Cary Nemeroff, Soke, 10th Dan
Fukasa–Ryu Bujutsu Kai

I have known David B. Nemeroff for a long time as his sensei and as his friend. From my perspective as a licensed and certified practitioner of the healing arts, and a fellow Aikidoka, I have followed the evolution of David's martial arts education. In this book, David presents his thoughts and practices in order to correct the misinterpretation of budo as taught in America today.

In the introduction he writes: "*This book was conceived in order to awaken the warrior spirit and revive the very foundations that made the martial arts so valuable…*" Regarding this spirit, O'Sensei Morihei Ueshiba, the founder of Aikido, gave Japanese budo a true and different meaning from other martial arts. Master Ueshiba stated:

Budo is a divine path established by the gods that leads to truth, goodness, and beauty; it is a spiritual path reflecting the unlimited absolute nature of the universe and the ultimate grand design of creation. Reform your perception of how the universe actually looks and acts; change the martial techniques into a vehicle of purity, goodness and beauty; and

master these things. When the sword of harmonization link-
ing heaven, earth and humankind is manifest, one is liber-
ated, able to purify and forge the self.

David B. Nemeroff's work is an invaluable source of knowledge for any serious budo student who is about to embark in this lifelong journey. I consider this book well–written, informative, practical, complete, understandable and right to the point.

The message is easy and crystal clear to grasp. The book is organized into twenty–one chapters, most of which focus on the essence of the moral and intellectual education necessary to the training of body, mind and spirit of the budoka.

He explores essential elements incorporated into bukiwasa and taijutsu practice and their application to promote personal development, peace, harmony and health. To achieve balance in budo, integration of theory and practice is vitally important.

After having read a preview of this book, I genuinely believe it is a great contribution to society and should not be ignored. The knowledge and practices herein will complement and enrich any martial arts practice. I have no hesitation in recommending Sensei Nemeroff's won-derful book. My congratulations!

Sensei Jose Andrade, M.D., USA Regional Director.,
Kyoshi (6th Dan) Aikido, Kokusai Budoin.
Director of Aikido Tenshinkai of Florida, Inc.,
Orlando Florida.

"I do not consider myself to be an authority or a master of the martial arts; I am just a person who enjoys the sincere practice of them. This book is a way for me to give back to the martial arts, since they gave me so much."

David Nemeroff

Introduction

Welcome to the exciting world of Aikido! Whether you are interested in finding a school or you are already a seasoned martial artist, *Enter into Aikido* will help to lay the foundations for training in the martial arts with the proper mindset. This book is simply an insight into the *Aikido–ka's* (practitioner of Aikido) perspective, leading the reader to evolve as he does. It is divided into two sections with the first part being a guide covering topics such as helping people to choose the right school and teaching them what can be expected as a beginner. However, as the reader delves into the second part of the text, the topics are meant as a guide for training the spirit.

Training can get you into shape, improve your confidence, and provide a fulfilling activity that can affect all aspects of your life. Although the martial arts are most well known for their methods of combat, this book was conceived to awaken the warrior spirit and revive the very foundations that made Aikido so valuable as a way of life.

I wrote this book to rekindle a tradition that has transformed men into masters of their lives and to share a philosophy that is slowly being lost by many modern martial arts schools today.

If you are only looking for quick belts, trophies, and a good workout, then Aikido may not be for you. In fact, there are no competitions in Aikido. However, if you are willing to explore a genuine paradigm shift in addition to improving your physical state, then Aikido can be an excellent choice.

The philosophies discussed in this text are not necessarily limited to Aikido, but Aikido is well known for its fusion of martial arts technique and spiritual principles of love and peace. These ideas may seem contradictory, but as an aikido–ka continues to practice, he comes to learn that true victory can only be achieved by attaining inner peace. By approaching conflict with this mindset, a dangerous situation can be handled with a calmness of mind and may even be diffused before it escalates too far.

Although I have studied several different martial arts, I chose to write about Aikido because I believe strongly in the positive message that it conveys. I do not consider it to be better or worse than other arts, but rather my particular area of interest and study because of its unique perspective and distinct movements.

This work can be a great resource for those looking to open their minds to a different perspective or a guide for potential students considering studying Aikido. Each individual dojo has its own way of doing things, but after training at several different schools and learning several different styles of martial arts, the subjects discussed within seem to be commonalities that are congruent amongst many of them.

Some of the information included in *Enter into Aikido* can be confirmed in other resources, but several of the ideas have come from great instruction and personal development through my own practice and research. The ideas in this text are not the only way to do things, but rather one of many that has been cultivated through personal experience. It is my hope that readers will integrate the ideas that are applicable to them, further enlightening their minds and adding another dimension to their training. After reading portions of the book, martial arts students should take these concepts back to the dojo and incorporate them into their own practice.

Throughout this text I use various Japanese terminology, so I felt it essential that I explain how to properly pronounce them. The pronunciation of Japanese terminology is different than it would sound in English. Here is how you would pronounce the vowel sounds:

A = "u" sounds like the "a" in father
E = "ay" sounds like play
I = "ee" sounds like see
O = "oh" sounds like flow
U = "ooh" sounds like boo

Finally, I discuss at length the essential nature of Aikido and the depths to which a person can be immersed into his or her training throughout the book, but newcomers should not be intimidated by its complexities. Lessons are not meant to be force–fed to students during training, but often realized as a *Eureka!* experience through the unrelenting repetition of technique. Aikido has no religious affiliations, and it is not a cult; instead, it is simply a way to personal development and defending oneself. A person can make his or her training as in–depth and/or spiritual (not religious) as he or she likes. Although certain explanations in this text are brief and may produce further questions, to find those answers, one must search for a knowledgeable teacher and train.

This book can never truly be finished, since a martial artist never stops evolving as long as practice continues. Although each chapter covers a separate topic, it was necessary to write about each of them as a natural progression of experiences in the dojo. It is your job to add your own chapters while reflecting on personal experiences that occur during your own training.

Section I

Starting Your Journey

Brief History of Aikido

One cannot talk about the history of Aikido without mentioning *O–Sensei,* or great teacher, Morihei Ueshiba. Ueshiba was born in Tanabe, Japan in December of 1883 and died in 1969. Originally a sickly child, he did whatever he could to strengthen his body. Not only did he work on the fishing boats hauling heavy nets and spear fishing, but he also took up swimming and got involved with Sumo wrestling. His impetus for starting his martial arts training happened after watching his father being beaten up by thugs. Because of this, he vowed that he would not let that happen to him.

As he got older, during his teen years, he began his training in several martial arts including Kito–ryu Jujutsu, Yagyu–ryu, Tenjin–shinyo–ryu in addition to Shinkage–ryu and Hoizon–ryu sword systems. In the early 1900's Morihei enrolled in the army, but was rejected due to his short height. He was eventually accepted, however, after incorporating a rigorous stretching routine including hanging from trees for hours with weights attached to his feet to gain the extra half–inch he needed. After enrolling in the army, circa 1904, he spent much of his time training other soldiers and was promoted quickly through the ranks. Eventually he was sent to the Manchurian front where he fought in the Russo–Japanese war. Around 1906, Morihei received an honorable discharge and returned home. Afterwards, about 1912, he moved to Hokkaido. During this time he developed his physical strength and martial skills further to a point where they were considered almost legendary.

It was also during this time that he met Takeda Sokaku, the Grandmaster of Daito–ryu Aikijujutsu. Takeda Sokaku was renowned for his prowess in combat and had many disciples interested in learning from him. Morihei was also very impressed by Takeda and so he built a dojo in Hokkaido and asked Tekeda to stay and train him. Ueshiba immersed himself in Sokaku's training and his teachings were paramount in influencing Ueshiba's martial arts and key in making what is now Aikido.

Ueshiba eventually left Hokkaido after hearing of his father's serious illness and so he headed back to Tanabe to be with him. It was around this time that Ueshiba called his art Aiki–budo. He left his dojo to Sokaku, and on the way an interesting turn of events happened. Instead of going directly to Tanabe, he made a detour to Ayabe where he met another extremely influential character in his development, Onisaburo Deguchi. Onisaburo was the head of a neo–shinto sect called the Omoto–kyo (Omoto meaning great origin) and the son–in–law to the lady founder Nao Deguchi. Within this Japanese religion there was a strong belief in *Kami,* or spirits, the power of nature, and focus on ancestral worship. Morihei took to him and his teachings right away, but to his dismay, he ended up staying there longer than expected and when he returned home his father had already passed. Devastated by this, he sold off his land and moved to Ayabe to delve further into the Omoto–kyo. Its lessons including the goal to unite humanity permeated his personal philosophy and his practice of budo. Ueshiba spent years with Onisaburo Deguchi, but eventually left to follow his own path. Throughout Morihei Ueshiba's life he continued to develop and teach his art to people of all walks of life in order to spread the message of peace and unity. In 1948 he passed his art to his son Kisshomaru Ueshiba, naming him

Doshu, or "Keeper of the way." Eventually, Morihei passed away due to illness on April 26th 1969, but Kisshomaru continued his father's aim to spread the art until passing it to his son, Morihei's grandson, Moriteru Ueshiba, circa 1986.

道場

Starting Your Search

Everyone has differing preconceived ideas about what the martial arts are and what their training will be like. This is why it is important to do some soul searching before you decide to begin this exciting journey. Whether you want to just get into shape or get the complete "traditional dojo" experience, there are a wide variety of schools and styles from which to choose. Therefore, make sure that you know what your goals are before you walk through the dojo doors, and do some prior research about which style of martial arts will best fit those goals. Try reading different books and exploring the Internet for resources, but realize that people can post anything on the Internet, so what you find may or may not be accurate.

Why did I choose the martial arts? There were two reasons really. First, my cousin and role model growing up studied the martial arts since he was five. I took any opportunity I could to see him, and eventually his enthusiasm permeated into me. I even remember one time where, as a youth, he took me to his dojo and I got to take a class. His teacher personally worked with me and although I do not recall too much of that day, I do remember stomping on his foot pretty hard while working on a self–defense technique. Whoops! He never told me that I was supposed to pretend and stomp near his foot until it was too late. As we got older, the weekends we spent together often started off with him bringing me to his basement for a training session. At the time, however, they seemed more like I was a punching bag than anything else. I soon realized it is as important to take a hit as to learn to give one. We did not have mats. Instead, we threw each other on a cement floor covered only by industrial carpeting, which hurt a lot. My jujutsu training during those days was some of the worst and, in hindsight, some of the best sessions that I had. It really started to toughen me up. Once I could not move anymore, we would turn on the "3:00 Saturday Afternoon Kung–Fu Theater" and laughed for hours.

Around the same time, I had a friend who carpooled with me to and from our weekly religion classes. Afterward, he would be dropped off at the local Aikido school for practice. For years, he invited me to come in, but it was not until one January in the early 1980s that curiosity got the better of me. That night I asked my parents if I could see what Aikido was all about, and after speaking to my friend's parents, they agreed. Although my parents did not do much research into the background and quality of other schools in the area, I was able to try a class. Because of my friend's recommendation, I was fortunate that it was a reputable school.

I have been training ever since, and I credit the martial arts for molding me into who I am today. They have made me a more confident, disciplined, and stronger individual, both physically and mentally.

Benefits at Any Age

If you are not a person in your twenties, this does not mean you should give up on your dreams to train in the martial arts. With time and conditioning, there is plenty that can be done, even for the older folks. Practice can be modified to accommodate those with physical limitations, so if you are interested in the martial arts, get in there!

Parents who are searching for children's classes may have different goals than those interested in adult classes. Unlike some adults who focus purely on self–defense effectiveness, traits like discipline, focus, and character development are also benefits that parents may be looking for. Parents should find a sensei who is good with children and takes an active role in their personal growth. This may include examining report cards and working with the parents to reinforce positive values both in the dojo and at home. Understand that it is unrealistic for a sensei to be the sole source of discipline in a child's life, rather he is a compliment to what the parents should already be doing.

A child's sensei should be stern but not a drill sergeant. This is because when discipline is taught in a harsh manner, children may instinctively resist it as a form of constant punishment. Instead, classes should be fun and exciting, while at the same time structured and regimented. Afterall, children learn through example.

Women in the Martial Arts

I am a firm believer that anything a man can do a woman can do just as well, if not better. This includes practicing the martial arts. With our world being filled with crime, it is extremely beneficial for a woman to know how to defend herself. Therefore, more and more women are enrolling in martial arts programs and proving themselves in the dojo. Women are seeing all that the martial arts have to offer and improving their physical and mental health in the process. Aikido is a great art for women because it teaches how to apply the laws of physics and use momentum so that it is possible for a smaller person to subdue a much larger one. Additionally, Aikido can give women a sense of empowerment and confidence that can extend into other areas of their lives.

Exceptions should not be made during class simply because a person is a woman. Men and women should be in the same class and do the same exercises. Men often underestimate women's abilities and so they pull their punches during practice, but this defeats the purpose of training and creates a false sense of security. I know that many men are taught not to hit a woman, but this is not the same thing; it is training. A real attacker is not going to be so nice.

When looking for a martial arts program, women should be cautious about taking a short–term "women's self–defense course." In order to become proficient enough to defend herself, a woman needs more than a few hours of training. Although these courses teach good concepts, they only give a basic exposure to the martial arts and, in some cases, the illusion that they are suddenly ready for battle. Consistent martial arts training is the only way that a person can learn how to effectively respond to an attack. Another consideration about many of these programs is that they often do not have men participating. Since most women are attacked by men, not other women, men should be active in a self–defense course in order to give a sense of realism. If a woman is serious about learning how to defend herself, she should find a credible school in her neighborhood and train regularly.

Unfortunately, there are some men that belittle women for studying martial arts. In our society, some men's egos may seem threatened if a woman is stronger or more able to defend herself than he is. These men will often say things like, "A woman could not really do anything against a man on the street because they are physically weaker." That is nonsense. I have seen women drop men twice their size with the right technique and the men were not just taking it easy. This is because Aikido is not only about strength and size, but also use the principles of physics including speed, power, fulcrums, and levers.

On a positive note, this attitude is starting to improve. If you are a woman considering martial arts training, do not let stereotypes, misconceptions, or other people discourage you. It will be well worth your while as long as you choose the right style according to your goals.

Common Concerns for Perspective Students

After watching the first class, you feel excited at the possibilities of what you can learn, but there are some concerns you may have about whether or not you should actually join. I know I had some when I started. One of these may be, "The other students look very graceful, but I am a klutz. Will I be able to do what the other students are doing?"

The simple answer is yes, you can. When you see the other students performing techniques well, it is only because they have practiced them repeatedly. In the beginning, most people start off feeling awkward and even the most skilled martial artists have those "special moments." The best thing you can do is just laugh about it and then move on. As you continue to train, you will become less of a klutz.

Another question that people have is, "Will I hold back the other students if they are more advanced than me?" Not at all. Remember, everyone started out as a beginner, so students are compassionate to that insecurity. The advanced students can still benefit from practicing with people of all skill levels.

I often hear the question, "how am I going to remember the Japanese terms?" By coming to class this will happen naturally. I also recommend bringing a notebook to class and writing them down afterwards. That way, you can bring them home and study them at your leisure. This is another example of how Aikido trains the mind as well as the body.

Some people also ask, "Will the falls hurt?" In the beginning there may be some discomfort, but as you continue to get thrown, that should subside. From falling during class, the body becomes tougher and more conditioned to handle the throws. Your falling technique will also improve over time, which will make the landing less jolting. Eventually, falling can be easy and some even find it enjoyable.

Choosing a Style

There is no such thing as the ultimate martial art, but there are several different systems to choose from. One of which will resonate better with the natural way you move and the philosophy by which you live your life. Understand that there are arts that focus on sport and tournaments, some that focus on self–defense effectiveness, and others that are mostly spiritual in nature. The techniques of each art are simply vehicles for applying the underlying theories that lead students toward a specific purpose. Some of the more legitimate styles you will encounter will have more than one of these aspects, so ask a lot of questions until you find the system for you.

Bujutsu and Budo

In Japanese martial arts, there are two main categories that can be separated into *bujutsu,* otherwise known as *bugei* (martial arts) and *budo* (martial ways). Bujutsu are military arts of combat and usually have the suffix "Jutsu." Some examples of these include Jujutsu (gentle art of war), Kempo–jutsu (fist law art of war), Kenjutsu (sword art of war), and Bojutsu (six–foot staff art of war). These arts were designed for combat effectiveness on the battlefield during war times, and so those who trained in bujutsu developed a warrior's mindset that was about pragmatics more than spirituality. Bujutsu arts were not only concerned with protecting the individual, but more importantly, put emphasis on group combat. Classical bujutsu *ryu* (styles) often incorporated several different areas of study, including various weapons and empty–hand methods preparing for all aspects of battle. This included applying those principles to all facets of daily life. As an evolution from the bujutsu arts, budo arts developed during a time of peace after the need for the samurai diminished and, therefore, focus more on individual spirituality and the attainment of self–perfection. Budo arts are those with the suffix "–do" at the end of their names.

Some of these include ways such as Aikido (way of life in harmony with internal energy), judo (gentle way), kendo (way of the samurai sword), and most commonly karate–do (way of the empty hand). Without exception, each true budo system comes from a bujutsu predecessor. For example, there was no judo before jujutsu, or kendo without kenjutsu. In budo systems, it is common to see focus on one particular area of study, and many of the killing techniques were removed to allow for safe practice without injury. With this being said, many systems of budo are still effective methods of self–defense with modern–day applications.

Bujutsu and budo can be further separated into classical and modern forms. According to Donn Draeger, a martial arts historian and authoritarian, in his book *Comprehensive Asian Fighting Arts,* classical bujutsu and budo are those that were really or conceptually created before the twentieth century with classical budo beginning around the eighteenth century. Any bujutsu and budo created starting in the twentieth century is considered as modern.

In reality, there are some gray areas as to the distinctions between bujutsu and budo. One could even say that once a bujutsu art is used for individual preservation and/or enlightenment instead of group warfare, it could be viewed as budo. Many masters would often call their bujutsu arts a budo because they agreed with the budo philosophy or because many of the people from the modern–day society could not differentiate between the two. Therefore, they would use the term "budo" to make it a more generic term that was easier to understand. For example, some aikijujutsu masters would also use the term "aiki budo."

Currently, a third category has developed, which is the martial sport. When an art promotes competition for titles, trophies, or rewards, it ceases to be a bujutsu or budo art. Again, bujutsu are designed for combat, not points. There are no pads, no rules, and no referees to stop the fight. A sport art is not a true budo either because a budo art focuses on improving oneself, not competing against another. Some sport arts have lost their effectiveness altogether, practicing only choreographed kata (pre–arranged forms) alone without the benefits of ever having a real attack. Whatever your interest may be, when searching for a school, decide whether you are looking for a bujutsu, a budo, or a sport system.

The following is a brief partial description of Aikido and a few of the many Japanese arts available. Weapons systems will be discussed further in the chapter titled "Weapons and the Martial Arts."

Aikido

The term Aikido is made up of three ideograms. The first "Ai" (pronounced like "eye") means harmony, the second "ki" (sounds like "key"), means universal energy, and the third, "do" (pronounced "dough") means a way or path. Together the three symbols can be translated to mean "A way of life in harmony with ki, or internal energy and the energy of the universe." Aikido has its roots in Daito–Ryu Aikijujutsu, which was the art of the Takeda Samurai family. There are various styles of Aikido, with Morihei Ueshiba being considered the father of Aikido and the person responsible for its widespread popularity and positive message. Although Ueshiba is known for the name "Aikido," it is interesting to note that some other budo/bujutsu instructors used the term Aikido pre–World War II before Ueshiba officially recognized it as the name of his art in 1942.

Aikido is the balance of *In & Yo* (positive and negative forces) and the unification of mind, body, spirit, and emotion. Aikido is moving Zen. It is the physical manifestation of spiritual principles encouraging the practitioner to constantly evolve.

Aikido is an effective means of self–defense, self–discipline, and self–mastery. Aikido is about harmony, not war. In everyday life, the aikido–ka must keep centered with calmness of mind like the eye of a tornado, because the chaos of life is always spinning around you. If you get caught up in its whirlwind, you lose control and get blown away.

It is also important to understand that the only thing someone can control is themselves, not his/her attackers, his/her surroundings, or situations that may happen to them. It is for this reason that we strive toward inner peace and, therefore, control of ourselves. Aikido is not a sport because there is no competition. Instead, the battle is the enemy within, and the goal is to achieve balance in every aspect of life. Although spiritual in nature, Aikido is not a religion and does not conflict with other religious beliefs.

The difference between Aikido and other martial arts lies mainly in its application of philosophy and spirituality more than its techniques. This is partially due to Aikido's emphasis on harmony and non–violence to resolve conflict. However, the ability to perform technique based on a three–dimensional sphere instead of a two–dimensional line, as seen in many other systems, creates a more profound and efficient method of defense. The unique footwork and unification of movement with an attack also provides a distinct method for maintaining control in a volatile situation.

Aikido as a form of self-defense

Aikido is based on physics, so when applying the principles of aiki (moving in harmony with internal energy), the practitioner can redirect the force of an aggressor, using it against him/her. The more force that is exerted by the attacker provides more fuel for the aikido–ka to perform a better evasive move and more powerful throw. The techniques of this art are performed in a totally relaxed, but not lazy, manner, staying fluid and free of rigidity, but still having structural support and power. Movements come from the hips, allowing for a balanced center and flowing movement.

There are many different techniques in Aikido, some may say an infinite number of them. There are techniques that manipulate the joints, some that immobilize the body, and others that project the attacker away, sending them flying through the air. What often makes an attacker go, is that they are in pain. The pain can be temporary or more permanent depending on how far the aikido–ka takes the technique. When executed gently, the pain is enough to control the attacker and force him into submission. When taken to extremes, an Aikido technique can damage joints and tear connective tissue. Other times the techniques work because the aggressor becomes over–committed in his movement and unable to regain his balance in time.

So, is Aikido effective? Yes, it is. There are skeptics out there that say it looks more like a dance and that the attacker is allowing the nage to throw him, but that is not true. Aikido, when done correctly should look effortless because the aikido–ka is moving with the attack, not against it. Others have said that they have seen aikido–ka who were not able to defend themselves, but that does not mean Aikido is ineffective either. It means that the individual's Aikido was ineffective; Aikido works just fine.

Some people have said that it is unrealistic to think that an assailant will just walk up and grab your wrist, so why are there so many wrist grabs in Aikido? The reason for practicing techniques from wrist grabs is two–fold. Firstly, a defense from a classical wrist grab is not the most practical, but that is not why Aikido is practiced in that way. Aikido–ka practice from wrist grabs as only one phase of training. It allows the nage to feel what the technique should feel like when done correctly, free from resistance. By doing so, he can learn the proper mechanics of the move. Then, once he has learned the proper method for doing the technique from a wrist grab, he can apply it to a more realistic attack from a strike, grapple or even a weapon. The second reason is that it teaches the uke how to fall for the throws in a safer way, minimizing the risk of injury for beginners.

Are there times when aikido–ka use strikes to defend themselves? Many styles teach that strikes can be a useful tool in the right situation. Other Aikido systems rarely use them. Strikes can stun an attacker, allowing the aikido–ka more time to put on a technique. Strikes can also loosen an attacker who is tense, rooted, or resistant. The strikes in Aikido are applied in a way that compliments the movement of energy, in order to off–balance the attacker further.

Some Aikido instructors exclude kicks in their Aikido practice, is this true of all Aikido? No, this is another common misconception. I have heard several rationalizations why kicks should be excluded, but there are more important reasons why kicks are a part of Aikido. One reason that I have heard is that we must always have two feet on the ground to stay centered and so kicking compromises balance. It is true that when a person lifts his leg, his balance becomes temporarily less stable than on two legs, but sometimes a kick is useful. There are times when a kick may be needed especially if your hands are already in use, so why restrict the use of an effective tool in our arsenal. As long as kicks are kept at a low level, they can be practical without sacrificing much. Besides, why would Ueshiba limit himself by "not allowing" kicks in his art? He probably would not have. Aikido techniques are said to manifest naturally through its movements, so it is possible that a kick could emerge as part of a defense.

Another reason why some instructors eliminate kicks during practice is because they feel that defenses against kicks are too dangerous for the uke. By this rationale, maybe other techniques should be taken out because they could potentially cause damage. If the uke is trained well to take good ukemi then he will be fine. Just because something is difficult does not mean it should be excluded. If the instructor is concerned with uke's safety then start off practicing the techniques slowly and increase the intensity as the uke progresses.

With more and more people studying martial arts like Karate and Tae kwon do the potential of a person attacking with a kick is becoming more likely than in the past. Therefore, it makes sense that an aikido–ka learns how to defend against one. By practicing kicks an aikido–ka is exposed to another level of training, better preparing him to handle them and use them if the need arises.

Overall, Aikido is an effective means of self-defense, but because of its complexities it can take longer to understand its intricacies and therefore may take more time to learn how to utilize it correctly. However once you do, Aikido can be a great ally should the need to protect yourself arises.

How are Aikido techniques different from the techniques of other arts?

Aikido technique is more than a block or a strike. The repertoire of throwing, locking and projection throws add another dimension to the martial arts. Although observing various Aikido techniques may superficially give the appearance that they are like the techniques of other arts, the way that they are executed are somewhat different. Aikido has blocks and strikes, however, upon a deeper exploration of its technique, there can be found some more advanced concepts that allow for a more efficient method of defense than striking alone.

In Aikido, when we are pulled we enter. When we are pushed we turn and when we are given a strike, we evade. For example, a joint lock like *kotegaeshi* (wrist twist throw) is not muscled into position by forcing the attacker into submission and aggressively twisting his wrist. Instead, the aikido–ka allows the technique to happen on its own.

The turning of the wrist occurs as a result of a spiral type motion. The spiral manifests through a combination of the nage redirecting and hyper extending the attack while the attacker attempts to compensate for his target suddenly not being where he thought he would be. Then, as the attacker recoils, he unknowingly set himself up for the throw.

Often new students describe the feeling of getting thrown with a good Aikido technique to having the nage suddenly not being there. It is like falling through a hole or going to sit down and having the chair pulled from underneath you. You expect something to be there, but then it is gone.

Another distinction of Aikido techniques is the circular movements within them. There are circles everywhere. They are in the footwork, in the hip rotations and in the arm and hand movements. Many times there are multiple circles within one technique. The circles provide a more dynamic execution, increased power and seem to help flow in harmony with a person's ki. At the same time, the circles make it more difficult for an attacker to anticipate what is going to happen until it is too late. This is much different than the linear approach found in other forms of martial arts.

During the execution of Aikido defenses, there is a constant awareness of one's center. Not only within one's own body, but in relation to the center of the person attacking. A nage's center is almost always at some point facing toward the uke's and by moving in certain ways, like *shukaku* (the dead angle), an aikido–ka can turn an opposing energy into a complimentary one.

Aikido techniques emerge by combining several principles of aiki movement, unification of energies and understanding anatomical composition. Those who study the techniques of Aikido realize that they also are stepping–stones to something more. It is only through experience can someone comprehend what that is and how they actually work. In reality, an aikido–ka does not decide which technique to use before being attacked, they are presented to him by the assailant as a natural reaction to the attack that is given.

Styles of Aikido

There are currently several different styles of aikido throughout the world. Many of the styles are the off–shoots of Ueshiba's art as taught by various students of his. Even though Ueshiba taught each of them, their Aikido differed slightly depending on the historic time period that they learned it and what the style focused on. This is due in part to Ueshiba's personal evolution of the art. Overall, as time went on, Ueshiba became more focused on the spiritual side of his art and so there seems to be a general trend of the styles of Aikido getting softer and more spiritual as the art progressed toward the present.

There are also other styles of Aikido that have a totally different lineage with no connection to Ueshiba at all. There is some controversy on whether or not a style can be called Aikido if it is not of Ueshiba lineage; however, one must first consider a few things. Firstly, the term and the practice of "aiki" were around before Ueshiba created his art. Secondly, the term "do" is simply a way or path. So it is conceivable that those who studied a jutsu art like aiki–jujutsu could have evolved their art using the name Aikido with no connection to Ueshiba. However, Ueshiba must be given the credit for his paramount skill and unique vision as well as popularizing the art and spreading its name.

Commonalities amongst Aikido Styles

As vast and different as they are, all Aikido styles seem to have commonalities between them. Firstly, Aikido's efficacy has a strong foundation in the dynamics of movement. When done correctly, there is no resistance between the attacker and the aikido–ka. Instead, an Aikido practitioner blends with the momentum of the incoming attack, redirecting it and ultimately neutralizing it. By moving in harmony with the attacker, the attacker defeats himself.

Next, Aikido has strong moral and spiritual teachings. Each style will have varying degrees that they emphasize this aspect of training, but most strive toward the evolution of oneself. The focus is not to dominate others but to positively affect those around us. Although it may seem contradictory to any martial discipline, Aikido is about peace and living in harmony with the rest of the world.

Thirdly, the physical techniques appear similar from style to style. There are joint–locks, hip throws, take–downs, and pins included in all Aikido. How a person enters into them, the angle that they are applied or the hand positioning may be slightly different, but the underlying principles are generally the same. As stated earlier, Aikido's fluid techniques derive power from creating three–dimensional circles. By doing so, it makes it harder for the attacker to resist while keeping him off–balance.

All Aikido uses ki. In fact, if there is no ki, then there is no Aikido. It is in the name after all. By adding this dimension to a martial art, a practitioner can gain a deeper understanding of himself, combat, and the universe. Without utilizing the power of the mind and the breath, all one has is superficial physical technique.

Pre–World War II vs. Post–World War II Styles

There seems to be a dichotomy with Aikido styles at the time of World War II. The pre–WWII styles are considered the "old–school" systems, whereas those emerging after the war are the "modern" traditional schools of Aikido. Pre–war schools are generally harder and more militaristic, while more closely resembling the "jutsu" wartime arts like aiki–jujutsu. Post–war schools commonly have more flowing and wider sweeping movements than their pre–war predecessors. Furthermore, in post–war schools there is more focus on spiritual, rather than combat, applications. It is not to say that pre–war schools are better or worse, or that post–war schools are ineffective, only that their approach to practice is often focused on two different areas. The list below mentions many of the major pre– and post–war schools, but is by no means a complete compilation of all the styles that exist. No style was intentionally meant to be excluded and all have merit.

Pre–World War II Styles

- Aiki–Budo: Aiki–Budo was the name of Ueshiba's style early on in its inception. It was not until around 1942 that he made the name Aikido official. This style is, as characteristic of other pre–war styles, harder and more focused on the martial applications.

- Yoseikan: Yoseikan Aikido, or "place where truth is taught" Aikido, was the name given to Minoru Mochizuki, circa 1931. Mochizuki not only studied Aikido under Ueshiba but had studied many different martial arts including judo directly under Jigoro Kano, the founder of judo. This system incorporated other martial arts such as judo and karate into its curriculum.

- Yoshinkan: Yoshinkan Aikido began in 1955 under Gozo Shioda. A student of Ueshiba, he began his training in 1932 at the age of eighteen and trained under his tutelage for about eight years. Shioda dedicated his life to Aikido and to his teacher. In Yoshinkan, there is emphasis on mastering the basic techniques through repetition as well as a focus on street combat.

- Ki no Kenkyu–kai (Ki Society)/Shin Shin Toitsu Aikido: Founded by Koichi Tohei, he put a strong emphasis on the development of ki (internal energy). This soft Aikido style is less concerned with the pragmatics of self–defense and teaches Aikido as a method of health and unifying man with the universe. Ki exercises are a regular part of practice.

Post-World War II Styles

- Aikikai: This is considered by many to be the main branch of Morihei Ueshiba's Aikido, which is currently governed by his grandson, Moriteru. The Aikikai seems to be more of an umbrella organization than a particular style because of the wide variety of backgrounds and training methods of its members. Some have a very basic curriculum with mostly wrist–grabbing techniques while others emphasize weapons training. Movements are often large, flowing, and almost dance–like. Aikikai Aikido is taught as a means of self–discovery and truth with a more pacifist philosophy.

- Fukasa–ryu: Fukasa–ryu, or "system of depth," was the name appointed to Cary Nemeroff, Soke, for his profound knowledge of many martial arts and advanced technical skill after decades of intense study. Fukasa–ryu Aikido is derivative of pre–war Aikido, and although it has many similarities to other Aikido systems, it is not of the Ueshiba lineage. The Fukasa–ryu's main concern is with combat effectiveness against real uncontrived attacks. All aspects of aiki and various weapons practices are incorporated into the training.

- Iwama–ryu: Iwama–ryu is the style originally headed by Morihiro Saito. Saito was the student who was considered to spend the most time studying directly under Ueshiba. Saito's Iwama–ryu was connected with the Aikikai although stylistically it is different because in this style there is a lot of focus on weapons practice. After Morihiro Saito's death in 2002, his son Hitohiro Saito formed his own organization, Iwama Shin Shin Aiki. It seems at this time that he became independent from the Aikikai, although some of Iwama–ryu's students rejoined Aikikai to keep that affiliation.

- Nihon Goshin Aikido: This art was founded by Shodo Morita in Hokkaido, Japan after studying several different martial arts including Judo, Jujutsu, Kobudo, Karate and Daito–ryu Aikijujutsu. Morita studied Daito–ryu under Yoshiro Kitaro and eventually combined his knowledge into order to have an art that utilized what he believed to be the best principles from each art that he had learned. Then, an American stationed in Japan by the name of Richard Bowe studied Nihon Goshin Aikido under Morita's tutelage. After Morita's death and his son, Nara Tominosuke retired, Bowe inherited the system. Because of this, currently there is no Nihon Goshin Aikido left in Japan.

- Mukei no ryu Aikido: After studying with several renown instructors of Aikido and other diverse styles of martial arts, Dr. Jose Andrade, Sensei's perspective has made his style unfold along a unique path. Mukei no ryu is his distinct "style without form," detached from the confines of system or form. At the highest level, the techniques are manifested through improvisation of the movement process and the harmonization of ki. Mukei no ryu Aikido embraces applying Zen principles to modern situations to make both a spiritual and practical art.

- Tomiki–Ryu/Japan Aikido Association: This art promotes the Aikido teachings of Kenji Tomiki. As a student of both Morihei Ueshiba and Kano, Tomiki wanted to combine the competitive aspects of judo and the spiritual philosophy of Aikido. He felt that since the art could no longer be tested in battle, competition was the next best thing. Therefore, both empty hand and knife competitions are common. However, Ueshiba disconnected from Tomiki because he felt that there was no place for tournaments in Aikido. Practice of Tomiki's Aikido is comprised of kata (pre–arranged forms) and randori (sparring techniques).

Other Non–Aikido Styles of Martial Arts

I wanted to mention other styles of martial arts because some of them had an influence on Aikido during its creation. However, not all of the arts mentioned below were involved. Below is a list of various Japanese and Okinawan martial arts.

Jujutsu

Jujutsu is one of the oldest empty hand martial arts of Japan. Its English translation means "gentle art of war," and it is a Japanese martial system that was utilized by the samurai (warrior class) when they were disarmed or if their sword was disabled. Jujutsu focuses on throwing and grappling, using subtle methods to uproot and off–balance an opponent. It is called "gentle" because of these subtleties and because it is efficient, not because it is soft or weak. In fact, like other forms of bujutsu, its techniques were developed through actual combat by warring samurai. Students of jujutsu learn more than sword disarming; they are trained to defend themselves and others against both unarmed attackers and aggressors with weapons of all types. Jujutsu practice includes ukemi (rolling and falling), shinki–waza (knee–walking), shimi–waza (choking techniques), nage–waza (hip throwing), kansetsu–waza (wrist and arm breaking), ne–waza (ground grappling techniques), and atemi–waza (striking techniques).

Kempo

Kempo, or "fist law," is an elaborate blocking and striking system that was designed to function alone or in conjunction with throwing systems of the same ryu (style).

Kempo's techniques for blocking and striking allows a person to enter into his opponent's space by parrying, deflecting, and moving out of the way, avoiding lethal strikes. This "opens the door" for limitless possibilities. Kempo–ka (practitioners of Kempo) can utilize these blocks and strikes to off–balance an aggressor, preventing further attack. The training in Kempo focuses primarily on efficient retaliation against attacks that are uncontrived. Practicing this art entails drilling blocks and strikes for proper technique, speed and power, and then applying it against a variety of opponents. There are systems of Kempo from China, Okinawa, and Japan.

Judo

Judo translates to "the gentle way" and was developed by Jigoro Kano. (On a side note, Jigoro Kano is the man who developed the Kyu/Dan ranking system, which refers to having various student and instructor ranks that represent ability and skill for the martial arts.) The art of judo evolved from the ancient combat system of jujutsu as a kinder method of self–defense, a way of life, and a sport. One main difference between judo and its predecessor jujutsu is that the more lethal jujutsu techniques were removed from judo, making it an effective, yet more compassionate art. Competitive judo also takes an opponent's weight into consideration, whereas jujutsu does not.

Exponents of judo use leverage, momentum, and an understanding of kuzushi (destroying balance) to perform a myriad of hip throws, sweeps, chokes, and joint locks. This art emphasizes throwing using the least amount of strength and energy possible, focusing on efficiency of the body. Part of judo practice is randori, a competitive exercise in which opponents attempt to throw and subdue each other until one of them submits. Judo has grown worldwide and has even been included as an Olympic sport.

Karate–Do

In karate, or "empty hand," the practitioner trains the body to be a weapon for unarmed combat. Through rigorous conditioning, the body is hardened in order to deliver a repertoire of effective blocks, strikes, and kicks. In addition, kumite–waza (fighting techniques) and kata (pre–arranged forms simulating combat) are incorporated in order to ingrain techniques into muscle memory. *Kobudo* (farm implement weapons) is also commonly a part of the karate curriculum. Karate originates from Okinawa and some more modern systems from Japan, but its earlier roots can be found in the Chinese martial arts. Within karate, there are different schools of thought varying from the hard to softer styles. In modern times, there are literally hundreds of different karate systems that have propagated throughout the United States and around the world. They range from the traditional older combat methods like Shorin–ryu and Goju–ryu to more modern "sport arts" that are designed for tournaments and earning points.

Choosing a Dojo and an Instructor

Once you have narrowed your search and decided which art interests you most, visit different schools to determine which one is right for you. Do not be afraid to travel a little farther to get good training. Definitely do not settle for a school just because it is close to your home or because it is a little less expensive. On the other hand, do not pick a school so far away that it becomes a hassle to go to class.

I personally used to travel three hours several times a week to train with my sensei because of the quality of training he provided. I still continue to travel around the country to this day. I know this is a little extreme for some, but it is worth it to me because I want the best education possible. Remember, you are making an investment into your future well–being and a possible lifestyle change, so you want to be sure to get the best possible instruction for your money.

Do not choose a dojo based on the name alone without first observing the skill of the instructor. Buying into a name is the same whether it is a car, a pair of jeans, or a martial art. I know that seeing commercials of four–year–old children breaking boards and women doing flying spinning kicks with promises of you being a warrior in six weeks can be exciting, but more often than not, the promises are a far cry from the truth. It is the product, not the name, which should determine what to invest in. Therefore, do not buy into the hype solely from a good marketing strategy. If a dojo looks more like a corporate brand than a school, you may be paying for a name instead of a martial arts education.

Find a school with Asian credentials. This is important because they help to validate that the information taught is legitimate, traditional, and not just made up by someone who attended a couple of seminars or watched a few videos. Would you send a student to a university that did not have credentials? Also, make sure that the certificate is not all he has. An instructor should also be able to back up his certificates with his skill during practice.

Another crucial thing to look for is how comfortable the instructors make you feel. Do you get a negative feeling from the school, or do you feel at ease when you walk through the door? A good teacher should make perspective students feel welcome (without bombarding them with a sales pitch or unrealistic promises) instead of a burden for wasting his time. When potential students come into my school, I always make it a point to introduce myself and have a member show them around. This reinforces the family–type atmosphere that I like to have while helping new students to feel less like an outsider. In fact, my students talk outside of class and enjoy monthly dojo dinners so students feel like part of a family and not just a customer.

Find out if the teacher will allow you to watch or try a free class. If not, he may have something to hide or be insecure with his abilities. If you were shopping for cars, you would not buy it without first taking it for a test drive, so why take that risk with something as important as your martial arts training? By watching the sensei, a person can assess his teaching style, and if the sensei has the working knowledge to effectively apply his skills. You can, most importantly, decide if the school is right for you.

Good instructors are humble, so beware of a sensei that has a big ego. Usually those who have to talk about themselves the most know the least. It is okay to be confident, but let their skills do the talking. If they are bad mouthing other schools, this can also be a warning sign because, although it is easier to tear another person down than it is to elevate oneself above the rest, it is not respectful. The martial arts are a method of promoting discipline, personal growth, and world peace; it is not a machismo contest. A true master has nothing to prove and no need to show off.

Choose an instructor that gets on the mat and participates in class instead of an "armchair sensei" who watches from his desk. If the sensei is always watching instead of training, what kind of message does that send? Doesn't a sensei expect you to train constantly and rigorously? Martial arts training takes work, and if a student does not constantly practice to hone their skills, his proficiency can quickly deteriorate. If teachers do not practice their own skills, they too can become rusty, so watch the teacher during class because learning from the "arm chair" sensei with less–than–perfect skills can produce less–than–perfect students.

Beware of teachers who promise you rank according to time instead of demonstrating the required skills. If students attain rank in this way, are they reaching their full potential? When a student is promised rank ahead of time, as many non–traditional schools do, there is no need for the individual to attain the necessary skill level required for that rank. This diminishes the quality of the martial art. When rank is given in this way, it turns the martial arts into a business venture instead of a method of self–defense and personal growth. By over–emphasizing the importance of belts, it is more likely a marketing ploy and motivational tool to keep you coming back and paying more money. Making martial arts your occupation is noble, but promoting students quickly in order to make extra money undermines what the martial arts are all about. After all, a belt is just a piece of fabric representative of the hard work a student has endured. By focusing on getting the fabric instead of the hard work, he has shown that his mind is not in the right place and is not focused on the spirit of budo.

For those who are looking for more than just a good workout, be cautious of schools that emphasize the winning of trophies or medals. I know that many people like competing and may even join a class for that very reason, but when there are trophies and/or points involved, it becomes a sport, not a martial art. Real martial arts were originally designed for survival, not material rewards. Ask yourself, "What is the big picture and the reason for training in the first place?" If the response is only for a belt or trophy, the training becomes skewed and the proper mindset is lost, compromising the effectiveness and intent of the art. Besides, if the whole objective is attaining a trophy, then is a student done training once they have won it? How many trophies or medals are enough? There has got to be something more.

Speak to the other members of the dojo. They were a potential student once, so they will have insight on some things that you may have overlooked. Ask if they still like the classes. Do they have a favorite instructor or class, and why? Is there anything that they dislike about the school? Also inquire if they previously studied at other schools and why they left. These answers should help you make a wise decision.

Lastly, do not feel that once you enroll in a martial arts program, you have signed your life away. It is all right if potential students are not initially ready to make martial arts their life's passion when they decide to register; if it is meant to be, that will happen naturally over time. It is more important to just enjoy the practice. Some students may spend their entire training being content showing up for only an hour or two and leaving without thinking about class again until it is time to practice the following week. A good instructor, however, can help spark the warrior spirit necessary to appreciate all aspects of the martial arts.

正統性

Lineage and Legitimacy in the Martial Arts

With martial arts schools appearing throughout the world with increasing popularity, a serious controversy has emerged for martial arts enthusiasts, old–time practitioners, and those prospective students who want to find an authentic school. The issue involves lineage and legitimacy.

Many potential students may feel that the lineage of a martial art is unimportant, especially if they only want a good workout or an after–school activity for their child. It can also seem overwhelming to do the necessary research when most people just want to have fun. So why take the time and effort to research a martial art's lineage? Keep in mind that it may not be important now, but after several months of training, you may find yourself getting more involved in the martial arts world and left wishing that you had those affiliations. Although there are no guarantees, by finding someone with a true martial arts lineage, it gives some assurance that the martial art is one of quality. It is better to start off on the right foot.

As a martial artist, it is important to have Asian–recognized credentials because it gives a sense of authenticity to a practitioner and their *dojo* (martial arts school) in a society where there is no governing body of martial artists to regulate what is taught. What are Asian credentials? Asian credentials are certificates or letters of acknowledgement given to a person, recognizing him at a particular rank. What differentiates these certificates from others is that one can only attain Asian–recognized credentials by studying a Japanese or Okinawan martial art with historic lineage. Furthermore, the certificates are usually given by a Japanese or Okinawan martial arts organization. They are considered like having pedigree papers, and it is believed that the closer one is directly linked to a teacher of the past means that the passing down of these ancient martial teachings will be more pure. Without them, it is hard to know the quality of information a student will learn and whether or not the system is authentic. It also means that martial arts instructors can teach whatever they choose in any fashion they choose.

By finding a school with Asian credentials, it provides some assurance that the instructor will have a certain level of knowledge. There is also a validation and respect within the martial arts community that comes along with having studied a traditional martial art. However, just because an instructor has the right credentials or is connected to the correct lineage does not mean that he is an effective teacher or the right instructor for you. It simply means that they studied a legitimate style. Therefore, a prospective student should meet the instructor and take an introductory class before agreeing to commit to a school. Consider though, if an independent sensei without current Asian credentials is skilled as a martial artist and a great teacher, it may still be worth learning from him.

Those interested in studying a traditional art should recognize that many schools today claim to teach "traditional martial arts" but use the term more as a catch phrase than anything else. Just because a person bows and says, "Yes, sir!" does not make them traditional. Rather, they must have ties to a bona fide Japanese or Okinawan family system and preserve the cultural practices historically associated with those martial arts. A dojo owner may not pick and choose which customs are convenient and still be considered legitimate. Moreover, an integral part of the martial arts experience is lost when those practices are watered down or if students do not understand why they are done in the first place. Eliminating the underlying lessons and formal traditions causes martial arts training to become a purely physical activity. Then it ceases to be a completely traditional art.

Over the years, I have heard my share of strange claims with reference to this very issue, but one story stands out above the rest. I received a phone call late one evening from a man who wanted some information about my school. After my usual greeting, he started to ask about which arts I taught at my dojo, which is normal enough, but things quickly took a strange turn. He continued and asked how a person becomes the founder of his own system. At that point I knew things were about to take a turn for the worse. I explained to him how one becomes a legitimate *soke* (head founder), but I had to ask him why he wanted to know. He then told me about "Raptor style."

"Raptor style?" I said.

"Yep, Raptor style. You know, like in the movie *Jurassic Park*." He then began to tell me how he had studied different styles here and there for about a month at a time and also watched different videos in order to make the ultimate martial art. He also wanted to incorporate my techniques into his style and apply them the same way that the dinosaurs did in the movie. I think I almost fainted. I stopped him mid–sentence because I did not want him to proceed any further. I politely explained that I did not want to be involved in that type of endeavor, but if he had an interest in studying a traditional martial art without pursuing "Raptor style" I would be happy to help him. I never heard from him again. This is not the way to become a legitimate martial artist, though it exemplifies why proper credentials are so important.

Legitimacy and Certification

The controversy over an art's legitimacy does not usually occur because of modern day effectiveness, but rather has to do with claiming rank and connection to particular arts. It is said that one way to determine legitimacy is to examine the age, its relation to Japanese history, and the ties one has to the art's original founding family.

Even if an instructor can produce a certificate, it is difficult for the average person to distinguish between what is legitimate and what is fraudulent. One has to examine who signed the diploma and the organization that awarded it, to see who his teacher is. Any stamps on the diploma may further explain what the lineage is. By having information like this, a person can trace his lineage back to see where the martial art came from and if it is a documented style. Some good resources are Westbrook and Ratti's book *Secrets of the Samurai: The Martial Arts of Feudal Japan* and Draeger and Smith's book *Comprehensive Asian Fighting Arts.* These are easily accessible books that give a good historic explanation of the arts as well as a list of several different authentic styles. Although they do not mention every system, they are a good place to start. A person may also want to contact martial arts organizations that are located in their country but have direct connections to Japan and/or Okinawa. They can often provide helpful advice for any questions that may arise.

Generally, the older systems known as *koryu* are considered to be some of the more respected of the combat methods. (Koryu is a Japanese term that refers to ancient Japanese martial arts. This word literally translates as "old school" or "old tradition" and relates to the schools of martial arts that predate the Meiji Restoration. The Meiji Restoration was a political event that facilitated Japan's modernization. There are also accepted budo methods that are referred to as Gendai budo. These are more modern arts that evolved from koryu methods. They emerged around 1876, after the time of the Meiji Restoration of 1868.)

The names, and more importantly the techniques, within a particular system are property of the *soke* (head of the system). As a side note, the word soke is used less often in Aikido than in other martial arts. Instead, terms like Doshu are sometimes used. One only becomes a soke by being recognized as a legitimate founder or by inheriting the system from the previous soke. Only that person can make decisions regarding the art and who can teach it. That person also decides how to best grow the *ryu* (style) and can choose a successor, or soke–dai. When people start to make false claims that they have a certain rank or teach techniques without the proper permission, it dishonors the art and essentially steals from the soke. Further, only approved sensei certified by the current soke of the art can use the name of the ryu to promote students. It does not matter how skilled a practitioner is because without the proper documentation and signatures a person does not have any proof that they studied an authentic bujutsu or budo system; therefore, they are not considered to have rank in that art by that organization.

Moreover, any certifications that were awarded are still considered to be property of the current soke. If a person leaves the organization, they may be asked to return their credentials. This is upsetting to some people because they feel that they earned the rank, but a certificate means that you are a representative of the ryu at a certain rank. If you leave the organization then you are no longer representing the art and therefore should not make claims to the contrary. With that being said, many organizations will allow students to keep their diplomas if they only have a student rank. This practice also prevents people from hopping from one organization to the next for the purpose of accumulating credentials. This is one reason why the ability to teach a legitimate system is an honor. If a teacher is in good standing with the previous soke, it does not mean that they will be permitted to teach by the current one either. Each member must maintain a practice with the best interests of the ryu in mind and train in accordance with the rules that the current soke provides.

After speaking to a person about his credentials, try and find other sources that corroborate their claims. If a person tries to avoid answering your questions, it is a warning sign that they may be a fraud. An authentic instructor will be upfront and give a straight answer. Do not fall for the "these are answers that I will share when you are ready" routine.

Proof of Skill and Credentials

While the above is true, and I have legitimate Asian credentials that prove my authenticity, I have to question those who are like me but spend their time trying to discredit or devalue the worth of another style or practitioner that is different from their own. Many times bad–mouthing will occur between instructors when trying to disprove the legitimacy of another system.

To have pride in a martial system when a person has dedicated his time and hard work is fine as long as it has not been taken too far. Remember, true *budo* (martial ways) and *bujutsu* (martial arts) teach acceptance, respect, and humility. It is understood that by having a traceable lineage, it protects potential students from a sensei who creates or changes a martial art in an irrational way such as having inconsistencies in martial strategies, illogical theories, and/or ineffective defenses. However, placing judgment on other systems without first seeing what an art is about is beneficial to no one. Everyone deserves respect for training sincerely.

Another thing to remember is that although documentation is important to prove legitimacy about a particular ryu, proper records were not always provided in writing. This can be confusing because if a family style was solely passed down orally from generation to generation, there may not have been written certificates or a need for them. Does this make it less of an art? This does not mean believe every claim, but perhaps give that person a chance to prove his skill; thus, you sacrifice nothing. Simply do the research instead of taking someone's word at face value.

Mixing of Styles

There are also the occasional dojos that teach their own mixture of styles, which they blend together. Beyond any historical and/or cultural implications, the problem arises when a person does not truly understand the philosophy and theory that fuels each of the original arts; thus, the result will be a non–cohesive and ineffective system. Just like languages such as German, Spanish, Japanese, or English, all of these are authentic and beautiful until you try to speak them simultaneously. Suddenly the compilation becomes incomprehensible. These stylists can give true martial arts pioneers a bad name and you may end up with another "Raptor style."

It was the sensei of old, like Ueshiba, who founded their martial systems after first spending years dedicating themselves to learning legitimate arts. For instance, Ueshiba first studied arts like Daito–ryu Aikijujutsu. It was not until much later that he expounded upon that information in a coherent way. Besides, many of the famous sensei evolved a pre–existing art into what they believed was the next logical step. They did not simply try to blend several arts together.

The problem of mixing arts is often the result of seminar hopping. Just because a teacher attends some seminars and has learned a few techniques does not mean that they are ready to teach them, and they definitely do not have the knowledge to create a whole system. To their credit though, at least most of these sensei are honest in telling others that they make their own mixes.

Fraudulent Promotion

Another, perhaps even worse, issue is that there are also those who promote themselves or are promoted by lower–ranking students; however, this is an illegitimate practice. This is illegitimate because just as a college student could not award his professor with a degree from their university, a lower–ranking student or black belt cannot give rank to his martial arts instructor. Similarly, there are groups of martial artists who like to cross train and then promote each other because they are friends. This is also fraudulent because as I stated earlier, studying a few techniques does not mean that you deserve rank. It takes constant training over a span of years to become proficient.

With this being said, how can we be sure who is legitimate? Ask for those Asian credentials, but do not let them blind you. Listen to their claims, but do not let them deafen you. Watch their performance of technique, and then decide if they are worth learning from. You may have found a gem of a teacher standing right before your eyes.

伝統

Traditional Martial Arts
in a Modern World

Things around us are changing all the time. There is a constant evolution that affects the way we live. Our society as a whole views things differently than it did only fifty years ago. This is true of the martial arts perspective as well. The question then becomes, "Do traditional martial arts fit into the modern world?"

Before answering this question, let's reiterate some rudimentary differences between traditional martial arts and their modern counterparts. Understand that these are not criticisms, because there is value in all different types of arts, both old and new. I am simply pointing out the distinctiveness of these two categories.

First, traditional martial arts were originally designed for use on the battlefield to break bones, injure joints, and even kill opponents; the focus is on combat effectiveness. Martial arts were designed for that purpose, and practitioners should continue to maintain that aspect during training. This not only includes maintaining physical techniques, but the preservation of the underlying strategic philosophies as well. They are, therefore, not well suited for modern sport competitions for obvious liability issues.

Practitioners of traditional arts do not use pads or gloves because people do not have the luxury of wearing them on the streets. Practitioners of modern arts, however, usually do. Many of the modern–day martial sports focus on aesthetics, acrobatics, trophies, and belts, all having to do with theatrics and material reward. Commonly, pragmatics is less of a concern since many competitions award prizes for flashiness over effectiveness. Even competitions like the Ultimate Fighting Challenge that claim to be "no holds barred," although more realistic than others, often have rules that restrict certain targets and techniques and require the competitors to wear gloves.

Some modern martial artists focus on competitive fighting and nothing else. Many of them practice "mixed martial arts," which is a little of everything mixed together and usually incorporates kickboxing, grappling, and whatever else is thrown in. They may be able to defend themselves, but eventually they will reach a point when the amount of new information diminishes. This is because only bits and pieces of various arts are taught instead of the complete methods of any one style. Traditional arts often have a lifetime of new information, or at least a progression that can span a lifetime for those who have the drive to attain that knowledge.

One should consider that according to budo philosophy, the goal is to prevent a violent situation from arising—not promote one. Therefore, the idea of a competition for the sake of entertainment, points, or money is contradictory to its principles. Traditional arts are more than just a physical activity or a gym class twice a week; they are a way of life with lessons that should permeate all aspects of daily living. Besides, what happens to the purely physical fighter when she becomes too old to fight?

Another difference is that traditional arts have a traceable historical lineage. Most modern arts are the creation of someone who has studied bits and pieces from various styles and mixed them in order to make it more marketable. By having a traceable lineage, there is a time–tested system, and as a result, reassurance of its effectiveness. There are other distinctions between the two, but this should paint a general picture.

One opinion is that traditional martial arts like Aikido are outdated nowadays because that type of training is too intense for the average person. In fact, I recently received a phone call from one woman who said she studied karate for several years. Her sensei was no longer able to teach, so she was looking somewhere else to train. When I began telling her about the arts that I teach and the underlying philosophy of the school, she told me that she was not looking for self–defense. Hearing that was disheartening for me because it is a reminder of where martial arts can end up if things do not change. The school that she attended previously only taught *kata* (forms), and that was all she wanted. Practicing kata is good, but when all that is practiced is kata, then it is less of a martial art and becomes more of an exercise or dance. Subsequently, I recommended that she look into a different school. I do not believe that traditional arts are too intense, because I have had five–year–old children and seventy–year–old women train and become successful. It is usually a combination of laziness and self–doubt that deters people, not intensity.

It is not easy to train, but it is very possible. It is simply a matter of conditioning. After the initial few months, the soreness will subside. The same thing happens when a person starts working out at a gym. One must be willing to explore outside of their comfort zone if they are ever going to achieve excellence.

Traditional martial arts, like Aikido, also employ proven strategies of combat. They have laid the foundations for many forms of self–defense, both armed and unarmed. As long as anatomy is the same in humans, the way in which they can be dealt with will be similar to how they were in the past. Jujutsu, for example, is a centuries–old system and still in the forefront of the martial arts world today. The theories behind traditional arts have been used in battles time and time again and are effective even now.

Technology and a "Fast Food" World

Some may ask, "What has changed that would make traditional arts obsolete?" One major contributor is technology. Actually, it is not the technology itself, because technology is neither good nor bad. Instead, it is the mindset it produces. Kisshomaru Ueshiba, son of the famous Morihei and the second *doshu* (leader) of Aikido, wrote in his book *The Spirit of Aikido:*

> Accompanying the dramatic developments in science, technology, and material civilization in modern times is the aggravation of the human spirit, which experiences restlessness, insecurity, and loss of direction. This is heightened by the threat of nuclear holocaust; mankind today stands on the brink of global disaster. (*The Spirit of Aikido*, Kisshomaru Ueshiba, 11)

Technology is improving at an exponential rate, making our lives more and more convenient every day. The Internet allows us to obtain limitless information with the touch of a button. We also have cell phones, fast food, and E–Z passes so we can do everything on the go. There is a constant push in our society to make things faster and less challenging, but before totally embracing this lifestyle, we must ask ourselves, "What is the cost?"

I would be lying if I said that I do not enjoy the many benefits that the modern world has given me, but I recognize them to be a tool, not the goal. People have developed an attachment to technology that has fostered the inability to perform simple tasks that they had been able to do previously. Too often I have heard people say that they need a calculator to perform simple math or children who cannot tell time if the clock is analog. Our people as a whole are losing basic skills because of the reverence toward our modernization. It is time to slow down and take an assessment of what is passing us by. Traditional martial arts can help to do that.

The "get it fast, get it now" mentality has permeated all aspects of our society. Play dates, business meetings, and other activities can distract us, and we are therefore in a constant state of running around, making no time for ourselves. In the modern world, there is rarely an appreciation for taking one's time to do something correctly instead of just getting it done. This attitude has affected the perception of the martial arts as well.

Chronic quitting is becoming an epidemic for students of the martial arts as well as many other activities in our modern world. There is a more prevalent "fast food mentality," with expectations of the quick reward with minimal work. This includes the expectation that because one pays tuition, he deserves a belt. When people realize that they actually have to put in hard work, many people quit and go in search of the next new and exciting activity. Kids switch from football to piano to martial arts like changing television stations. This produces "a jack of all trades, and a master of nothing." Many parents reinforce this behavior under the auspices of raising a well–rounded child, but what their children learn is that when something is difficult or boring, it is okay to quit instead of working through the issue and committing until the task is done. Ask yourself, "How will this attitude affect a child when he enters the workforce?" and "What type of work ethic will he have?" Conversely, this elevates the dedicated student to attaining something few others have achieved.

As mentioned earlier, people expect to pay for belts instead of earning them, acting as though it takes too much time to earn it the old–fashioned way. There are instructors who compromise their teaching to accommodate these people, and they earn good money doing it. The downside is that giving in to these pressures deteriorates the quality of real martial arts. This becomes more evident from the "McDojos" popping up across the nation and the number of black belts that those schools produce annually. To be a good martial artist, one must dedicate sufficient time, and no amount of money will change that.

Aikido teaches commitment in a fast food society. By always going fast, one can never enjoy the present because there is a constant focus on the future instead of living in the here and now. However, the philosophy of Aikido coincides with the idea of living in the moment and taking pride in one's work, moral character, and way of life. Therefore, it is not that traditional arts do not belong; rather they are needed more than ever.

Discouragingly, modern arts are often watered down to make them more marketable. The benefit of Aikido is that it teaches people to take pride in everything that they do, because what they do is a reflection of who they are. By living in accordance with Aikido doctrine, a person can enjoy their life instead of watching it pass by like an onlooker seeing it second hand.

Moral and Ethical Teachings

Another reason why traditional arts should not be discounted for the modern world is their moral and ethical teachings. Many families today have both parents in the workforce in order to make a living. Unfortunately, this often leaves children to fend for themselves. The lessons of life are taught to them through their peers or on the streets instead of through the guidance needed from constant parental supervision. Traditional martial arts, on the other hand, provide a strong moral foundation for our youth as well as positive role models for them to take example from. Experience has shown that students who participate in Aikido are better prepared to deal with the issues that may arise. They are more focused, are motivated to perform better in school, and develop ethical decision–making skills. These are characteristics that people can benefit from no matter what their lifestyle is.

Practitioners of traditional arts observe certain customs and rules of conduct of that culture, preserving the mindsets of those who practiced during ancient times. Many teachers of the modern arts discard what they believe to be unnecessary, like dojo etiquette and other formal practices. By eliminating this aspect of the martial arts, many mental and spiritual lessons that teach discipline and respect are lost. Some modern schools may dismiss requiring a uniform, give belts as an enticement to re–enroll, and disregard the importance of performing a bow, which is one of the most basic acts of courtesy. However, the martial arts should be a complete experience in order to gain the complete benefits.

Business and Interpersonal Relationships

These strategies can also be adapted to how we do business and how we view our interpersonal relationships even in the modern world. The moral and ethical implications of Aikido as applied to how one conducts business can mean the difference between creating long–lasting positive business relationships and engaging in shady dealings and developing a bad reputation. The fundamental tactical martial principles demonstrate that rather than facing a larger opponent head on, in business and in Aikido, one must exploit their weaknesses. In practice, many companies do the same by looking at the inadequacies of their competitors' products and/or services and develop better ones.

As it relates to personal relationships, Aikido promotes the development of character and an emphasis on appreciating all of life. Mutual respect, self–control, and humility can facilitate a healthy relationship and allow for the sharing of ideas without feeling threatened by those different than our own. This includes being open to one's teachers, and those who have shared their love with us, and that there is an obligation to help those in need. By maintaining a calm mind, an aikido–ka also learns how to deescalate emotional situations and promote a sense of peace. The tactics of traditional arts are truly timeless.

Where Does Aikido Fit In?

Aikido is distinct because it is a contemporary martial art rooted in classical Japanese budo. It may even be a bridge between the modern and the traditional. Historically, Aikido is not a very old art, with Ueshiba's Aikido being officially created in the early 1940s. However, since this art evolved from much older arts like Daito–ryu Aikijujutsu it has distinct aspects congruent with other traditional martial arts.

Aikido's traditionalism is evident in its strict code of conduct, which is found in other budo and bujutsu systems of Japan. Aikido–ka are taught how to bow, act, and train just as in any other traditional dojo. This includes wearing the traditional *gi* (uniform), *obi* (belt), and *hakama* (black baggy pants).

As stated earlier, a traditional art must have a traceable lineage, which Aikido does, as well as the proper mindset. Many Aikido systems maintain a focus on practical self–defense and, therefore, do not use pads during training. There is no competition and no need for medals or trophies. Aikido is still a martial endeavor.

On the other hand, some of Aikido's philosophical teachings are more progressive from a martial arts perspective. An aikido–ka is more interested in making peace than war. He has no need to dominate others, only better himself. A few Aikido systems have even gone to extremes and strayed from combat all together, focusing on the "art" aspect of training. Understand that this is not usually the case, and many Aikido systems are still an effective means of defense today. A practitioner of Aikido wants to grow physically, spiritually, and emotionally while being a positive influence on those around him. It is a respect for all life and a compassion for others that gives Aikido its modern flare.

Since Aikido is a fusion of the traditional and the modern, it may have the best of both worlds. It can provide order to those who feel like they have lost control of their lives and give confidence to those who feel helpless. Aikido was a dynamic method of self–defense to those of the past and still used by people around the world today.

The Future

What is the future of the martial arts? One can only speculate. Since there is currently no regulating body in the United States, the martial arts, if left unchecked, will likely change from what they were first intended. There may be an increasing dichotomy between the traditionalists, the martial sport participants, and the modern martial arts practitioners. I believe that as time passes, the martial arts market is becoming flooded with schools, causing the quality of martial arts to degrade in order to cater to the masses. Another potential outcome that seems to have already begun is the perpetual opening and closing of dojos, which causes students to jump from one school to the next. This could produce a melting pot of martial arts styles and result in phasing out traditional arts except for a select few. Some believe that creating a federal governing association to prevent the deterioration of the arts may be the answer. Although we do not know what the future holds, something must be done to correct our current problem.

Traditional arts can provide order in a chaotic world. The training that they provide helps center the mind, reduce stress, and give us a sense of purpose to something bigger than ourselves. Traditional arts create a family–type atmosphere that can provide a sense of belonging while strengthening bonds between people. With crime at an all–time high, these systems of self–defense can provide an edge in keeping our families safe and an overall sense of confidence that can improve the quality of life. Although some advocates of modern martial arts believe that it takes too long to earn rank the traditional way, I say that it is the information, not the rank, that is the prize. By giving up on traditional arts, humanity is losing a major piece of history and a beautiful art form.

Trust in traditional martial arts because they can provide the balance needed to have a healthy lifestyle in today's fast–paced world.

予期

What to Expect
as a Beginner

The first time I walked into a dojo, my nerves felt like pins and needles, and my heart was racing. I had no idea what to expect since I was an introverted preteen that barely weighed more than 100 pounds, short, self–conscious, and asthmatic. It seemed like the odds were stacked against me. I was already a timid child, and now I was entering a realm that was completely foreign to me. I did not know what to expect, let alone how to defend myself against people twice my size. Was I in over my head?

I did not have a uniform or a belt, so I stuck out like a sore thumb in a sea of students in full attire. I saw students being thrown across the room and pinned to the floor. I thought, *That is going to hurt,* and I was not sure if I could survive having those things done to me. Before I knew it, I was being led onto the mat.

Although the sensei was initially intimidating to me, he surprisingly understood my fears and began to put my anxiety at ease. I was not an athletic child by nature, but as class ensued, I quickly found myself doing things that I never believed possible. I felt awkward, but I was rolling, taking basic falls, and I even successfully put someone into a wristlock. The workout was challenging, but not impossible. As a result, my fear transformed into enthusiasm as the class continued. By the time I finished class, I was hooked. I knew I wanted to learn more.

After class, several of the other students came over to introduce themselves and asked if I enjoyed the class. I was exhausted, but I sure did. It was nice to have strangers make me feel so welcome. They continued to reassure me that I would be fine and recounted some stories of their first classes. The sensei then called me over and asked me what I thought of the class and if I would like to return. I told him that I would like to, but I wanted to discuss it with my parents first. The sensei did not pressure me or make me feel guilty; he simply said that I did a good job and that he hoped to see me in the future. I signed up the following week and have been training ever since. This was not only my experience as I have found that many other beginners have had similar experiences as well.

Preparing the Body

With television and cinema at the forefront of today's culture, the perception of the martial arts is becoming more and more skewed. Special effects and flashy jumping, spinning, and flying kicks can give prospective students a cinematic illusion instead of an effective practical reality. Martial arts are not about glory or money; they are about cultivating oneself with a lot of sweat and hard work. This is why it is important to understand what to expect once the decision to pursue the martial arts has been made. Although the rewards of this pursuit are sometimes subtle, they can change a person's entire way of life.

Aikido training can strengthen the body, open the mind to new ideas, improve flexibility, and increase both endurance and cardiovascular function. However, like any physical activity, Aikido training can put a toll on the body, especially in the beginning. Before starting any training, beginners should make sure that their bodies are healthy and can handle the extra activity. If you are unsure about whether or not your body can handle it, consult a qualified physician. Prior to taking martial arts lessons make sure that it is not a contraindication to your health.

New students often like to eat right before class, but this is a really bad idea. If you want to get some energy before class, I suggest leaving several hours in between to digest. The following story will explain why: I had a classmate who ate a plate of spaghetti before class in order to get more energy for his black–belt test. He was put through a grueling series of exercises, attacks, and trials of his technique and endurance. Needless to say, he made it through his test, but his spaghetti did not. After the test, he ran to the bathroom and the rest is history. So remember, the moral of the story is not to eat before class.

After bowing in to class, expect that the sensei will lead the class through warm–ups of some kind. These can include stretches to improve flexibility, calisthenics, meditation, and *ukemi* (falling and rolling).

It is necessary to practice the warm–ups at the beginning of every class to help maintain body integrity as well as provide a safety protocol that prepares students for the rest of class. The instructor should spend enough time on warm–ups to condition the body without making the class about aerobics instead of martial arts. Beginners may not always be able to keep up with some of the warm–ups, but that is okay. By regularly attending classes and continually practicing, they will gradually see improvement and catch up to the other students.

Warm–ups can be just as exciting as the rest of the class if they are treated as a method for challenging the body and focusing the mind. By neglecting the warm–ups, one may not be able to continue training as they get older and become more prone to injury. Even young people can have problems due to not warming up first.

Stretching

Stretching is very important in maintaining soft tissue health. Quite often, people suffer from stiffness, muscle soreness, neck, and lower–back pain—not necessarily from Aikido training, but from everyday life. This is frequently caused because of hypertonicity of the muscle fibers and/or tendons and ligaments, plus muscle adhesions and scar tissue. When one of these issues arises, it can restrict movement and pull the body out of alignment. Muscles control bone, so if the muscles are not soft and pliable, they may negatively affect posture and gait. An aikido–ka knows that posture is essential to good martial arts, so by stretching, we can allow for more fluid motion and increased range of motion. Additionally, a person who stretches regularly can move more quickly since he is not inhibited by soft tissue restrictions. All areas of the body can be stretched, and I recommend a minimum of a half an hour in the morning and before bed daily to maximize flexibility.

Here are some simple stretches that can be incorporated into your routine. Remember, all stretches should be done with slow and consistent pressure. Trying to do them quickly or with a jerking motion can actually cause injury instead of benefit. Increasing the range of motion through stretching should be performed gradually over time, taking the stretches to the point of discomfort, not to the point of pain.

Neck Stretch

This stretch can be done either standing or in seiza (seated position). Start by keeping the back straight. Reach over your head with one hand and place it between the ear and temple. Next slowly pull the head laterally to the side. If you are pulling with your right hand, you should feel the stretch on the left side of the neck. As you are pulling, it is important to continue abdominal breathing while visualizing all the muscles in the neck softening or melting. This will help the muscles to relax. Hold the tension of the stretch for about ten seconds and then slowly begin to release the head back to the upright position. Do not release the neck quickly. Once the neck is straight, wait five seconds and then continue with the opposite side. Repeat as necessary.

The next neck stretch is a forward flexion stretch. First, put your hands behind your head and interlock your fingers. Secondly, place your hands toward the base of the skull and gently pull down so the chin touches the chest. As you pull down, remember to exhale. Hold the stretch for about ten seconds, and then slowly release pressure. Once the neck is upright, wait for five seconds and then repeat.

Wrist Stretch

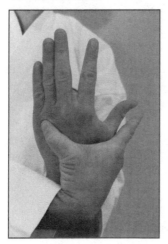 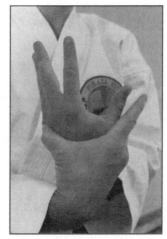

In the martial arts, the wrists are often twisted and manipulated in various ways, so stretching the wrists is important. The first wrist stretch is the "*kotegaeshi*–wrist twist." Start with the right palm facing you at eye level. Place the left thumb on the back of the right hand between the second and third knuckles. The remaining fingers grab the thenar eminence, which is the muscle underneath the base of the thumb. Next rotate the hand against the wrist until you feel the stretch. Then slowly release. Repeat this stretch several times and then go on to the opposite hand.

Another wrist stretch is for wrist flexion. Begin by placing your right hand palm down in front of you. Take the left thumb and place it over the right thumb knuckle and proceed to grab the pinky side of the right hand with the remaining fingers. Once the hand is secured, bend the wrist, bringing the fingers toward the forearm. At the same time, think about bringing the elbows together. After holding the stretch for approximately eight to ten seconds, release the stretch, bringing the hands down in front of you. The wrist will then be in a wrist extension.

Back Stretch

For the back, we will start with a back flexion–extension stretch. First, stand with the feet parallel and slightly wider than shoulder width apart. As you bend forward, exhale out of your mouth with the body hanging naturally. The breath should end about the same time the back is fully flexed. After the breath is finished, continue to hang, allowing gravity to assist with the stretch. Take one more inhale through the nose, and then exhale again while visualizing all the back muscles relaxing. On the next inhale, begin to stand up, rolling one vertebra at a time until the body is erect. For the back extension, place the hands on the hips with the thumbs toward the front of the body. Begin the extension by leaning straight back. Once the breath is completed, hold for another breath and then return to an upright position.

For a lateral stretch, place the feet parallel, wider than shoulder width apart. Start by pointing the left foot toward the left and bend the left knee so it is over the second toe. Shift your hips to the left while raising the right arm over the head and bend laterally with the back to the left side. At the same time, reach with the right arm. After holding the position for eight to ten seconds, return to an erect posture by first shifting at the hips and soon following by pivoting the left foot straight. Continue by pivoting the right foot toward the right to repeat on the other side.

Leg Stretch

When leg muscles are tight, it not only restricts the ability to kick, but it can also create low back pain. This is because the attachments for the leg muscles attach themselves to the hips. If one or more is in spasm, it can negatively affect posture, alignment, and gait.

To stretch the hamstrings, which are toward the back of the legs, start by squatting down, sitting back on your heels. Once this is done, extend one leg to the side with the toes pointing upward. To intensify the stretch, bring the head toward the extended knee. To stretch the other leg, keep the heels in place and shift the weight to the opposite side by moving at the hips.

Once the class completes the initial exercises, the main portion of the class can include a wide variety of topics. A well–rounded education can include defenses against different strikes and/or grabs, and at higher levels can also include weapons. There may be a focus on foot-work, since the feet and legs are the foundations of the body, or instruction in proper body mechanics and how to off–balance an opponent. Workouts should be rigorous to increase physical stamina. When practicing with a part-ner, the pace should be challenging, but not impossible. As a student progresses, so should the pace because she will be able to react more efficiently in response to faster attacks. Eventually, a senior–level student should be able to confidently and effectively defend herself against any number of full–power attacks.

Initially, it is common to feel some muscle soreness and/or minor stiffness, similar to the soreness of working out at the gym. However, over time the body will become conditioned and the soreness should subside. During this time, there is a tendency for some students to quit because they feel unable to cope with the initial physical stress. Do not give up; it will get easier. However, if there is constant or intense pain, it may be indicative that a more serious injury was sustained. In these rare instances, notify the sensei immediately. She is not a mind reader and will need to be informed of any problems and/or injuries that occur. Do not ignore an injury either. This may only compound it and increase the recovery time and result in time spent away from class.

Even when an injury is sustained, continue to observe the classes without physical participation. Although the physical training is temporarily postponed, the mental lessons can still continue by spending time at the dojo and simply listening and observing. Once the body heals, the physical activity can resume.

Preparing the Mind

Recognize that Aikido is not only about training the physical body, but also about developing the mind. The sensei may have students meditate as a means to calm the mind, conquer their fears, and contemplate their own personal and spiritual beliefs. By being open to these experiences, the martial arts can bring about an unexpected but welcome life change.

Be sure to attend classes regularly—"How can you learn an art if you do not show up to class?" Whatever the reason for starting in the first place, that goal can never be achieved if you do not show up to class. It is easy to make excuses like, "I will just go next time," or "I'm too tired," but one missed class can turn into two and then four and so on until eventually, "My schedule is just too busy to fit in training." Make the choice to train and then stick with it. Two or three hours a week is something that everyone can spare if they budget their time wisely. Moreover, the benefit from these couple of hours can have a profoundly positive effect on overall health and outlook, making the time spent worthwhile. When a student only attends classes sporadically, it keeps her from advancing her skills because she constantly has to review the old information in order to remember it. It also wastes the instructor's time if she must constantly repeat herself for this reason.

Repetition is crucial. I know that acquiring new techniques can be exciting, especially for beginner students, but it is only through the repetition of a technique that one can start to understand it and ingrain it into muscle memory. Forget about belts and learning new techniques all the time; instead work on perfecting the information at hand. Live in the moment and appreciate the knowledge that was given to you. When the time is right, the sensei will teach you another technique. Besides, from a purely self–defense point of view a person only needs to perfect five or six techniques to be effective against the average attacker. Also, a good sensei has no desire to keep his or her students from attaining rank. It is the student who truly determines how long it will take for them to receive new information. Unfortunately, many people want the quick and easy reward. Although it may feel like you are not progressing fast enough, you are where you are supposed to be. Some students may contemplate quitting when they find out that it takes more time and commitment than they expected, but the problem with that is a person can never become a master of anything if they are constantly giving up to start something new. This is one of the first mental tests of the aikido–ka. The intrinsic beauty of a craft, whether it is the martial arts or architecture, can then become watered down or even lost if never pursued to its fullest potential.

Another step in preparing the mind is through *misogi*. Misogi is the ritual cleansing of the body, mind and spirit. Traditionally, misogi may consist of chanting, meditating while using *mudras* (representative hand positions) or washing the hands and mouth during purification ceremonies. It can also include putting the body through extreme discomfort in order to learn how to block out the physical pain while centering the mind. Misogi may include meditating outdoors in winter cold conditions or relaxing the mind in extreme heat. Aikido can also be a form of misogi because it is said that constant practice cleanses the spirit. Eventually, any repetitive practice can be considered misogi if controlled breathing and clearing the mind are done in the process. Even cleaning the dojo can be a form of misogi.

Obtaining Rank

Earning a belt can be an exciting achievement and an important motivator for students. It is a way to set goals and gauge overall ability. As time progresses, a student should realize that it is the information learned while wearing the belt that is important, not the piece of fabric. The belt itself is only a symbol for the hard work and dedication given by the practitioner. Therefore, focus on perfecting the information, not the piece of fabric holding up your pants. Also understand that paying tuition does not obligate the teacher to give out rank. It must be earned.

Let me explain how the Japanese/Okinawan ranking system works. In many cases, martial arts systems were passed down from the father to the firstborn son. Within family systems there were not necessarily any written records of attendance or an archive of techniques until later on. Only the strong systems would survive because the practitioners of the less effective systems were often killed during battle, which resulted in the loss of his knowledge along with his life. It was truly "survival of the fittest," with less concern for titles and belts.

Most people are familiar with the wearing of colored belts, but they did not come about until much later in Japan's history. When indicating rank became more important, but before colored belts came about, there was a Menkyo, or a licensing system to signify one's rank. Within different ryu there are variations of titles and licenses; here is one example. Licenses may be titled Menkyo Shoden (lower–level student), Menkyo Chuden (middle–level student), Menkyo Joden (upper–level student), Menkyo Okuden (entrance to secrets) which was similar to first degree black belt, Menkyo Kyoshi (full instructor), Menkyo Shihan–Dai (sub–master), Menkyo Shihan (master–level title), Menkyo Kaiden (given to someone who has full proficiency in the art and knows all of its secrets) Soke–Dai (the one who will inherit the system when the soke dies), and soke (head of the family). Only one soke can govern the system. In the past, he was most likely the head of a samurai family, living to protect his feudal lord. Today, he directs with the intent to promote and grow the *ryu* (style).

It was not until circa 1880 that white and black belts came into existence thanks to the father of modern–day judo, Jigoro Kano. He is accredited with inventing the Kyu–Dan ranking system. Students are considered the kyu ranks or Mudansha, and the instructors are dan ranks or Yudansha. There are usually between six to eight kyu ranks, depending on the specific ryu, ten dan degrees, and one soke and soke–Dai, which for all intents and purposes are considered above all ranks so that they are able to promote to tenth dan. Understand that an instructor can only promote someone to one rank level lower than themselves. This makes sense because how can you grade another individual at the same level as yourself?

Furthermore, there is a difference between earning a rank and a title. For example, an instructor could have a sixth–degree black belt, which is his rank, but his title could be sensei, shihan, renshi, or something else depending on the organization. A title is a separate appointment above and beyond a person's rank.

Interestingly, although different kyu and dan gradings were developed by Kano, there was not the spectrum of colors for each belt like there is today. Instead, Jigoro Kano's Kodokan (the place founded in 1882 as a place to study Judo) had only white belts and black belts. There are different speculations on why the different colors came about. Some say it was because as the belts became worn the belts began to change color until, through experience of training hard, the belt eventually turned black. However, although this reason for the addition of colors seems a possible explanation, there is no historical proof to support it. Another more likely belief is that the use of colors was actually developed by the skilled judo instructor, Mikonosuke Kawaishi. Kawaishi taught judo in France and developed these colored belts in order to gauge the progress of students.

According to traditional Japanese practices, many organizations will not award a legitimate black belt until sixteen years of age. This is because a black belt is a symbol of maturity, sophistication, and motor control, which a young child does not yet have. Consequently, be wary of schools with lots of little black belts running around. To compensate for the age restriction and allow for the exceptional minor, there are probationary "Shodan–Ho" (junior black belt) ranks, which change to full black belt status upon the child's sixteenth birthday. Even with probationary ranks, a child still requires years of practice before legitimately wearing a black belt of any kind.

The Testing Process

The testing process is a time when students are challenged both physically and mentally in order to measure their growth as a martial artist and as a representative of the ryu. Tests can consist of almost anything related to the martial arts and vary widely depending on the style, the student's rank level, and the teacher. For example, a karate test may consist of *kumite* (fighting practice), performing blocks and strikes and demonstrating *kata* (forms), whereas an Aikido exam may include performing various throwing and joint–locking techniques and defenses against weapons. Tests often include exercises that challenge the student's endurance to the limit in order to see whether or not they will give up. Although some parts may seem like a physical trial, they may actually be a mental one as well.

Students often do not know what to expect during their test, so they may feel nervous before the exam begins. However, the feelings of anxiety are also part of the test. Just as in a fighting situation, a student must maintain control of his emotions so he can react calmly with a clear mind. If the student can do this, he is more likely to succeed. If his nerves get the best of him, he may forget his techniques or terminology and potentially fail. Before a test, do not dwell on passing or failing. Instead, go into the exam as you would any other day for training.

Consider that the test is just as much for the student as the teacher. A martial arts instructor already knows the ability of her students, otherwise she would not have invited them to take the test. "So why have the test in the first place?" you may ask. It is in part because it lets the student know that she can do it and therefore gives her confidence for when a real situation arises. It also lets the teacher know that her students are willing to persevere even when things get tough. Testing also gives an instructor the opportunity to correct and refine things that a student needs to improve for the next rank.

Motivation and Improvement

As a student, one has to search within to find the necessary motivation. If a student is bored it is usually because they are not viewing the lessons from the correct perspective. That is not to say that there are no poor quality schools that teach information in a confusing or boring way, but generally, if we look for it, there is always something new that can be learned. For example, postures can be improved, while footwork and techniques can always be refined. If after twenty–three years of training I can find ways to improve and keep my practice fresh and exciting, you can too. Remember, there is always something that can be worked on; all one needs to do is take the initiative to look.

When a student tells me that they have nothing to improve, they are not being honest with themselves, or more often they are trying to get new techniques before truly understanding the previous ones. For those students, it is important to just enjoy the process. To help with boredom, students should set realistic goals. Whether it is becoming more combat effective with their current repertoire of techniques or developing a better state of mind, setting goals can direct un–channeled energy into a more productive result. Over time, the lessons of Aikido should permeate into a student's consciousness and help the student to motivate herself.

Train with *shoshin* (beginner's mind). To practice with shoshin means to perform everything from etiquette and warm–ups and techniques to cleaning the dojo with passion and spirit. All tasks should be done as if it is the first time the task has been done and the last time that person will ever be allowed to do it again. Therefore, a person should carry out every task in its entirety with 100 percent of her focus. The concept of shoshin is not only about the activities in the dojo either. It is about doing everything in life in this way. By living with spirit, we strive for excellence.

After being at the dojo for a while, there is often a phase when students seem to plateau in their learning curve. During these plateaus, it may appear to a student like they are not learning anything new or they may simply feel a sense of stagnation in their training. Students often feel frustrated or even like they are getting worse during these times. This is common; however, by working through it, students can move forward and ultimately gain a better understanding of the art. Unfortunately, it is during this time that many students decide to abandon their training because of frustrations and/or insecurities. They should consider these transitions as a time to reflect inward, while working to refine the techniques that they already have. Consider a plateau to be a period of mental growth that can challenge students to cope and work through their issues of ego.

In the martial arts, when teachers promise rank merely for showing up for a month or two of classes, it gives students the wrong idea about training. Just showing up does not mean the information was assimilated and, therefore, does not necessarily mean that they deserve the rank they are given. Put in the hard work, and it will pay off. The martial arts are not a short–term endeavor, so keep your long–term goals in mind. Each class is a stepping stone that gets you closer to them if you stay on the right path.

Furthermore, it is not the job of the instructor to motivate you. Training is considered a symbiotic relationship where the student must take the initiative to motivate herself. That is her part in creating a successful martial arts experience. The sensei's job is to pass on the martial arts to her students, while keeping the system alive for the next generation. Those who are the most motivated, not rank driven, will progress more quickly than those who are not.

Dojo Etiquette

Another aspect of training is dojo etiquette. There are rules of conduct for each school that should be followed. Understand that by enrolling at a particular school, a person is accepting all of its policies, so she should make sure she is comfortable with them first. Some dojos will be strict and methodical in their observance of the rules while others are more relaxed during class. Choose the setting that fits you best. I personally believe that in order to be successful and get the most out of the martial arts, discipline is essential. I have found that to have respect for dojo etiquette is a sign of a disciplined mind and therefore a possible indicator of how a student may progress. (Dojo etiquette will be discussed further in a later chapter.)

Lastly, expect that your perspective about training will change as all things in life eventually do. Everyone's experiences will be different so do not try to compare yourself to others. Also, do not be afraid to speak to your teacher regarding any questions you may have. She will be more than willing to point you along the right path. When in doubt about your own training, revisit the beginning lessons in order to rediscover your initial enthusiasm. Forget about the pressures of earning the next belt and simply practice without ego or expectation. Live in the moment without judgment and have fun.

子供達

Children in Aikido

Children today are bombarded with violence in the movies and in video games. This is evident when we observe children imitating the moves of the Power Rangers, Ninja Turtles, and Star Wars films. When parents see their children acting in this way, they should consider signing up the child for a martial arts program. Parents may feel hesitant to do so out of fear that their child will learn violent or aggressive behavior, but a good Aikido program can actually teach children to control those tendencies in a healthy way. Parents may also be afraid of injury, but many more injuries result from traditional team sports than from Aikido training. Plus, Aikido can help parents to keep their children off the streets and equip them with the proper skills to defend themselves. Aikido and children is a match made in heaven.

So at what age should children begin Aikido classes? Although there are different opinions on this issue, I believe a child can start around five or six years old.

Around this age, they can begin to focus for about an hour and pick up basic movements. The study of Aikido can lay a strong foundation for a child's future, and I have even had students at this age defend themselves when bullies attacked them. There are "Little Dragon" type schools that teach younger children, but be careful before signing up with one of these programs. They often teach classes that incorporate a lot of tumbling, running, and yelling, which are great for expending lots of energy, but they are more like glorified exercise classes or daycare than actually learning martial arts. Once the child is old enough to focus, Aikido can be a rewarding and fun activity.

An Outlet for Energy and a Positive Influence for Children

There needs to be a positive outlet for children that can take them off the couch and mold them into successful contributing members of society. This is where Aikido can help. First, the physical challenges of Aikido can provide increased endurance and greater coordination and help children to lose weight. Over time, training can improve reflexes, reaction time, and agility. It can also help a child overcome certain physical limitations. It has personally aided me in managing my asthma through physical conditioning, meditation, and breath–control techniques. I have seen it help other conditions as well.

Since children have pressures at school, both parents are usually working, and crime is increasing everywhere, today's youth has an uphill battle in order to become focused and self–motivated individuals. Technology like the Internet and television can also spoon feed information to children, facilitating a lack of creativity. To my surprise, when I have asked some of my younger students to use their imaginations they responded with only a blank and confused stare because they said they never had to use it. Sedentary children are an epidemic, and the occasional football game with friends does not cut it.

When students train in Aikido, it is not to destroy another person; it is to help one another grow. They are not taught to develop confrontational attitudes, nor do they try to look intimidating. This is partially because an aikido–ka attempts to develop a harmonious relationship with their surroundings and the other people around them. This is an important lesson, especially for children.

Furthermore, what differentiates Aikido from other sports is that it helps develop ethical decision–making skills and reduce stress. Children are filled with what seems like limitless energy, and Aikido can help channel it in a constructive manner. An Aikido student learns how to respect his friends, family, environment, and himself. Aikido cultivates interpersonal relationship skills that are neglected in the public school systems and by our society. They also become more conscious of safety for themselves and others.

Growth and Confidence without Competition

Aikido has no tournaments or competitions except for the competition with oneself to evolve. Children will have enough competition throughout their lives, whether it is in school, on the playground, or in their future adult jobs, so there is no need to compete in Aikido. Aikido–ka work to better themselves, and by doing so, they will become motivated to continually progress and overcome the challenges in other parts of their lives.

There is no need for trophies or medals in Aikido either. The reward is the information taught and the positive changes that occur. Aikido emphasizes humility, and so as a child progresses through the ranks, he/she will develop a sense of accomplishment and confidence without the need to belittle others. When these lessons are applied to other aspects of their life, there is no limit to what they can achieve.

Unlike some other martial arts, aikido–ka do not break boards, bricks, or ice. Although that can be fun and build confidence in youngsters, breaking can be detrimental to childrens' health because their bones and connective tissue are soft and not fully developed. Breaking objects can cause long–term problems later on in life, and since I have never seen or heard anyone attacked by a board, there may be more constructive endeavors.

Children need stability and balance during their youth in order to mature into well–adjusted adults, so it is extremely beneficial when the lessons of the dojo are reinforced at home. Parents should, therefore, be involved with their child's dojo experience. When parents communicate with the sensei about their child, the instructor becomes more informed, and they can all work together for the benefit of the child. A good sensei will be happy to help in any way possible and can sometimes provide a disciplinary program for children who misbehave, but remember that a sensei is not a therapist or a disciplinarian. Additionally, parents should share the child's triumphs as well as any discipline problems.

Aikido is a constantly evolving art, growing with the student as he or she progresses. It teaches the body and mind to work together efficiently since the mind controls the body. When I taught in Brooklyn, New York, I came across several children who at seven and eight years of age were going to therapists, and some of them were on behavior–controlling medications. They had to schedule their play dates between German lessons, piano classes, and swimming while being toted around by their nannies, or as the children called them, "their other mothers." This saddened me because they had no time to enjoy just being kids.

One student in particular was brought to the dojo by his father with the goal to try and control his Attention Deficit Disorder and hyperactivity. This child was on Ritalin and threw frequent temper tantrums during class. Determined to help this child, I continued working with him while teaching him Aikido. Amazingly, he started to change. He no longer threw tantrums or screamed at the top of his lungs during class; he was content to be learning. I think he realized it too. The icing on the cake was when his father told me how his son's therapist noticed considerable improvement in all aspects of his life, including an 85 percent increase in assessment levels. I attribute his improvement not to me, but to Aikido.

Today's youth is an untapped resource, which, if caught early enough, can make a difference in the world. My sensei, Dr. Jose Andrade, M.D. once wrote:

> Youngsters have unlimited potential for learning. When they are motivated through Aikido,

they become reachable and teachable. If participation starts at an early age, the young student
will learn and retain beneficial attitudes and
behaviors. Why would parents have their trea-
sured child practice a martial art whose environment endorses and produces aggressive violent
behavior? Angry and unhappy young people, if
left unchanged, can become angry and unhappy
adults. Aikido's goal is not to conquer, dominate,
overcome, or eliminate anyone. Its objective is to
develop and refine the child's ki for an optimistic,
happy and active life.

By learning to follow a sensei's instructions, abiding
by the dojo rules of conduct, and embracing the teachings
of Aikido, a child is provided with the tools to mature
into a disciplined and focused leader of tomorrow. By
embracing Aikido, a child can also be a compassionate
and enthusiastic individual today.

生徒

The Role of the Aikido Student

"A teacher can only point the way to knowledge; the student must choose to walk the path."

What is the role of the ideal student? Is the goal of the student just to learn technique or are techniques a physical manifestation of spiritual ideals guiding us to live a certain way of life? Is simply paying tuition and attending classes enough?

The average student waits for the teacher to motivate her, but the exceptional student motivates herself and even inspires her peers. The average student must be reminded of the importance of coming to class, but the exceptional student needs no reminder and instead shows up without excuses, even when it is the most difficult.

Attitude

As a beginner, I believed the student who stood tall in line and performed techniques flawlessly might be considered the perfect student. Although the student who does this should be commended for her hard work, this is only one piece of the puzzle. The problem with students who are only interested in physical technique is that they lose sight of the bigger picture and therefore an essential part of their training, which is attitude.

Attitudes are like sounds that resonate through the dojo; they can be uplifting and powerful or heavy and disruptive. A student should practice with sincerity and selflessness. By doing so, the deeper spiritual aspects of the art can be discovered because ego is no longer in the way. Furthermore, when students have a positive attitude, they think of others before themselves, perpetuating the dojo as a place of mutual respect and learning instead of being a place for competition and machismo.

Shoshin

Ideal students train with "*shoshin*" or "beginner's mind." Many times the student who demonstrates shoshin will often surpass the physical achiever. This is because the student with shoshin perseveres relentlessly until her goal becomes a realization. Unfortunately, it is much harder to find a student with the right attitude. Any student can perform a technique proficiently with enough practice, but without the proper attitude, the student will be incomplete because all things physical deteriorate with time. This does not mean there should be no emphasis on physical training, but there should be a balance between the two.

Intensity

When on the mat, students should bring intensity to each class. By training with a realistic intent, it better prepares the *nage* (person performing the technique) for a potential attack outside the dojo. By only practicing casually, students lose the ability to defend themselves effectively as well as some of the mental acuity that develops from training in this way. Training with intensity also pushes us to go beyond our comfort zone and grow. Conversely, when a student has little or no intensity they become stagnant. Understandably, there will be times when students do not feel well physically or mentally, but as long as they put all of their remaining energy for that day into their training, their training will still be beneficial to them.

Quality vs. Quantity in Training

It is easy for a student to get caught up in the "technique hoarding" mentality, trying to gather technique after technique, kata after kata, and belt after belt. More and more beginning students believe they deserve techniques and/or rank at a fast pace just because they pay tuition, and some even become angry when these things do not come quickly enough. These students are the least ready to be given more information. They did not earn it, nor do they have the mentality to handle it effectively and with humility. Remember, it is not quantity, but the quality of training that should matter. If a student is taught a lot of information too quickly, there is no way for her to retain any of it. In fact, a student needs sufficient time between new techniques in order to integrate them into her muscle memory, making sure that each one can be done as a natural reaction that appears in times of need without thought.

There is an old proverb that talks about a student approaching his sensei.

> The student asks his teacher, "How long will it take to get my black belt?"
>
> The sensei responds, "I can't say."
>
> The student then insists, "I must know!"
>
> So the teacher replies, "Maybe five years."
>
> "What if I train for three days a week? Then how long will it take to get my belt?" the student asks.
>
> The sensei, disheartened, shakes his head and says, "Maybe ten years."
>
> More overzealous, the student asks one more time, "What if I train every day, then how long will it take?"

"Possibly fifteen years," says the sensei.

Confused and frustrated the student questions his sensei. "I do not understand. I say I will train more and more, sensei, but why do you tell me that the time to get my black belt will take longer and longer?"

"The answer is simple. The more focused you are on the piece of fabric instead of the practice, the further it takes you from the original path, and it will take that much longer to bring you back." A belt is just a piece of fabric if there is no sweat and hard work behind it.

Let me tell you a story about Steve. Steve was a student of mine who was similar to others I'm sure many teachers have seen walk through their doors. When he first watched a class, he said, "I'm ready to train hard because I want a black belt in the martial arts," which was good, but he was already focused on the material reward. Steve signed up for a year and bought all the necessary equipment. Meanwhile, he said he wanted to come to as many classes as he could fit into his schedule. The first month or two were great for Steve because he had never done anything like this before. Then around the third month or so, Steve realized that it was hard work. This was discouraging for him because he was looking for some instant gratification and did not get his belt yet. He did not realize that in order to be skilled at anything it takes dedication, commitment, and lots of repetition. If he did, he was not ready to actually follow through with it. Steve grew bored, not because the classes were dull or slow-paced, but because he gave up and lost sight of the goal.

Like all of life, learning happens in cycles. There are highs, lows, and times of plateau. A student with a good attitude understands this. What Steve did not realize is that every class can be fresh if he makes it that way. Take a technique that has been executed time and time again and look at it objectively without ego. Steve should have asked himself, "How can I make this better?" and made it happen. "The only limitations someone has are the ones they put on themselves, so break them down and push beyond them" (*The Dragon Doesn't Live Here Anymore: Living Fully, Loving Freely,* Alan Cohen, 128).

Next, Steve added another activity to his schedule to satisfy his fix, and his attendance in class decreased. He said he would try to make it into class one week, but "trying" is another term for "not being motivated enough," (Cohen, 49), and he never showed up again. The problem is that his negative attitude started to snowball until Steve decided to quit and take the easy way out. Maybe the martial arts were not for him, and if that is the case then I hope he finds something better suited for him, but this behavior seemed to be reflected in many aspects of his everyday life, from his work ethic to his relationships. Students like this usually do not like to take responsibility for their actions and will blame the teacher or other external forces for their lack of enthusiasm.

Conversely, the dedicated student is probably a hard-working and committed achiever in all aspects of her life, making sacrifices now because she knows she will benefit later. The hardest part of motivating oneself is that initial step, because like in the laws of physics, things in motion tend to stay in motion, and the opposite is also true. If a student takes a break from class, it becomes harder and harder to return because things at rest tend to stay at rest, contributing to complacency. This is one reason why it is so important to train regularly.

Role of the Sempai (senior students)

Along with being a senior student, comes added responsibility. Since they will be the future instructors, part of that responsibility includes guiding the beginner students along their journey and helping them to acclimate to the dojo atmosphere. The sempai should introduce themselves to new students on their first day so they feel welcome and less like an outsider. They should also show them where to get dressed, how to put on their uniform, and how to tie their belt. By initially giving them a positive experience, the sempai can inspire them and start them off on the right foot.

A sempai should volunteer to train with beginners. A good sempai realizes that she was once a beginner and so she must extend compassion and courtesy to everyone and a little compassion can go along way. She provides guidance during class and sets an example of what should be done. This is not an opportunity to demonstrate how much she knows or how little the beginner knows. Rather it is a chance to help new students in a new environment. During practice there should be minimal talking, so the sempai should demonstrate through her actions and let the new student experience the art instead of constantly correcting her verbally. Besides, the correcting of technique is the job if the instructor.

The sempai looks out for the welfare of the dojo. When a sempai is made aware of an issue, it is her job to bring it to the head instructor. The sempai is the eyes and ears of the dojo. Her job is to help the dojo run smoothly so by letting the sensei know of anything that may be going on, she could potentially help diffuse a more serious problem.

Keeping the Arts Alive

On a larger scale, a student should train to keep Aikido alive for the next generation. A teacher cannot do this alone, because eventually she will die, and the art will die along with the teacher if the information is not passed onto the next generation of students proficiently. Therefore, students must train with consistency and intensity to maintain the level of excellence that existed when the art was conceived. This way they can receive this wealth of knowledge correctly. If a student does not practice in accordance with these ideals, the art becomes watered down, changed, or even lost. As a result, the role of the student is also to help her teacher to spread the art. This includes doing demos, recruiting new members, and any other task that maybe required of her. This should be done voluntarily and willingly without expectations of reward, because helping the teacher is ultimately helping herself.

Although I was awarded a high level rank and title, I am also a student continuing to learn from my teachers. I plan to study for the rest of my life. As a senior student, I am often asked by my teachers to travel, do administrative work, or research in order to help them. This is just the way of things, and I am happy to be a part of it.

Students should respect their teacher because she has traveled a long and arduous path. She is the one who makes everyday people into martial artists, and so without her, a student's transformation would not be possible. Appreciate her. What students often forget is that the dojo is a symbiotic relationship; it is not simply a school owned by the teacher for the teacher's sake, but it is for the students as well. For success, the teacher must share her knowledge, and the students must accept it with trust, enthusiasm, and an open mind. Without both the students and the teacher there would be no dojo, so take pride in your dojo because everyone owns it in their own way.

道場

Dojo Etiquette

One reason traditional martial arts are taught with such an extensive code of conduct may be because they are a window into the Japanese culture, allowing people to see a glimpse of how the samurai viewed the world. However, a martial arts class can be a life's pursuit or a fun activity for a couple hours weekly, so do not let the etiquette or other formalities deter you from starting an Aikido program.

In a traditional Aikido dojo, etiquette is interwoven into every aspect of the martial arts experience. In Japanese, the word for etiquette is "*reishiki.*" This term can be broken down into its separate parts, the first being "rei," or to bow, and "shiki," which means a ceremony. So reishiki literally translates into a bowing ceremony or etiquette.

Rules of Conduct

From the time a person enters the dojo until the time he leaves, there are proper rules of conduct that must be followed. In the beginning, some students may feel overwhelmed or lost when trying to remember it all, but after coming to class a few times, they will quickly learn what is needed to perform it correctly. When in doubt, be courteous. By observing the code of conduct in the dojo, the class becomes more structured. This ultimately makes students more aware of their surroundings and provides a higher level of safety when training.

Depending on the individual school or style, the reishiki will vary. Traditionally, variations in reishiki could be due to the different spiritual beliefs of the soke or the time period in which that particular style of martial art was created. The geographic location of where the art was created could also play a part. However, no matter how different the etiquette is, its relevance is the same. Reishiki is a sign of a civilized person with good manners. People with good manners can often give the respect needed to appreciate this side of the martial arts along with its more profound teachings.

Some may ask, "Why do we have to perform reishiki in the first place?" The reason for this is simple. First and foremost, it is an act of courtesy. It is important that we show respect for the dojo, the teachers of both past and present, and ourselves. What many people do not realize is that by including reishiki, students can leave the problems of the outside world at the door and get into a more focused frame of mind as we enter the dojo. How completely a person embraces these acts of humility and accepts the importance of performing reishiki may reflect how far along the path to spiritual enlightenment one may be. Performing the etiquette correctly is a demonstration of a person's spirit and what is in their heart so others can often perceive their sincerity or lack thereof.

Reishiki is the fiber that keeps the martial arts alive. In order for a person to claim that he is studying a legitimate martial art, they must have the discipline and focus to respect all parts of its tradition. If this part of the training is not incorporated, then the student is simply going to a gym class to learn a couple techniques. After all, it becomes a contradiction to strive for the harmonious unification of the mind and body when the mental aspects of training are ignored.

As stated earlier in the chapter "Starting Your Search," there was a difference in etiquette between bujutsu and budo. The ritualistic spiritual practices of the martial arts did not become as significant until the emergence of budo, which came later. This is not to say that bujutsu exponents did not practice a codified set of rules for conducting themselves, but a student of bujutsu was concerned more with combat effectiveness than ceremonies. Generally speaking, the rules of the warrior had more to do with conduct in public and engagement in battle. Another distinction that effected martial arts etiquette is that the samurai spent much of their practice outdoors. Since there were no formalized schools for the martial arts yet, and as a result no shomen (front wall of the dojo), kamiza (small shrine at the front of the dojo), or other aspects of proper dojo design, some of the etiquette regarding dojo behavior did not come about until a period of peace arose.

During peace time, the necessity for the samurai became less. This caused the *bushi* (warrior class) to utilize their skills in other ways in order to make a living; consequently, many of them opened dojos. Since they were not constantly in battle, they had more time for other pursuits. Although there is some debate on which religions were the most influential, many teachers embraced the philosophies of Eastern religion and incorporated them into dojo life. It was then that the martial arts transformed from a mainly pragmatic system of defense to a more spiritual undertaking.

Along these lines, Morihei Ueshiba discovered the Omoto–kyo, a Shinto religion, which contributed to his personal growth and the development of Aikido. He incorporated its spiritual beliefs and etiquette so that Aikido could be a method of attaining enlightenment while providing a way to live in harmony with the universe. Aikido is not a cult or religion, but the teachings that were integrated into Ueshiba's Aikido provide the basis for creating a martial art of peace and mutual respect.

Here are some rules of conduct that one may find at a traditional Aikido school.

Bowing

Bowing is an essential part of dojo reishiki and has different connotations. In Japan, bowing can be used as a greeting. When a person bows in the martial arts, it is not a sign of worship, so there are no religious conflicts or implications to this act. Instead, it is a sign of respect similar to a handshake and is considered to be a part of having good manners. Bowing is not a sign of weakness either. Instead, it shows strength of character, as does any act of good etiquette. Bowing should be done with complete focus on the action and not on the other things going on around us. A similar comparison would be that a polite person would not shake hands with the president of a company while focusing on a computer screen.

Within Aikido, there is both a standing and sitting bow. The standing bow or "*ritsurei*" is performed from a natural posture, with the hands at the side of the body. As the bow is executed, the upper torso is bent approximately thirty degrees forward. The back and neck should be straight, in line with one another, with the fingertips sliding to the thighs, right above the knee.

When bowing to a teacher or someone considered of high rank, eyes should be looking downward to show humility. However, when bowing to someone in order to commence sparring, self–defense, or kata, the eyes should look forward at our opponent as a way to show respect while maintaining a sense of awareness.

The first time to perform a standing bow is while entering the space, in order to show respect for the dojo. As an act of reishiki, it is important because it sets the tone for the rest of the class. It allows us to regain our mental focus and proceed with a clear mind. It is also a chance to forget about the problems of the day. A standing bow is performed next when stepping on or off the mat. Bowing as we enter the training area also shows respect for the dojo as a place of enlightenment and learning. While entering or leaving the training area, face the *kamiza* (upper seat) when bowing. The kamiza is a place of distinction in the dojo that can be decorated with calligraphy, flowers, a sword, a picture, or painted scrolls. It is also generally an area reserved for the chief instructor of the dojo and guests of distinction like a visiting master. Another time to perform a ritsurei is before starting and when finishing the training session with a partner. As stated earlier, this is similar to a formal handshake that shows mutual respect for one another. Lastly, when leaving the dojo, a standing bow is done to compose ourselves for re–entering the outside world while honoring the dojo and the lessons taught inside.

Another type of bow is the *zarei*. The zarei is a more formal ceremonial bow and is done from a seated position. Preparation for this is done by first kneeling down on the left knee with the right knee up at a ninety degree angle. The toes of the left foot should be curled back.

Next, bring the right knee down so it is even with the left. This is *seiza,* or formal seated position. The toes should be flat, with the big toes crossing each other. The knees should be two fist widths apart, and hands should be on the thighs with the fingers together and pointed slightly inward. The back should be straight.

Once in seiza, we can begin the actual bowing process. Start by placing the right hand down on the mat centered approximately six inches in front of the knees. The left hand follows, and the hands are placed together to form a triangle.

Once this is done, bend the chest and trunk of the body forward so that the back and neck are in a straight line. When bowing, it is considered bad form in the Asian culture to bow the head lower than the body, exposing the nape of the neck to the people facing you. The head should come close to the hands but not touch them, and the hips should remain seated and connected to the heels.

A zarei is done at the beginning of class with students facing the kamiza to begin training and at the end of class to close the session. After everybody is in seiza, the chief instructor turns and faces the kamiza. He will then give the command "Yoi!" (assume the ready position) and then follow up with "Rei!" as a signal to bow. Afterwards, the sensei faces the students and then the command "Sensei–ni–rei," (bow to the sensei) is given. After the bow at the beginning of class, the students respond by saying, "Onegai–shimasu," meaning "May I practice with you?" Furthermore, at the end of class when the formal bow is done, the students respond with, "Domo arigato gozaimasu," or "Thank you very much for letting me practice with you."

Take Your Shoes Off

One of the first things we do when we enter the dojo is take off our shoes.

This concept not only applies to the dojo, but is also practiced in Japanese homes as well. The most basic reason for doing this is for hygienic reasons. By taking off our shoes, we stop germs, dirt, and other toxins from being spread throughout the home and/or the dojo. However, there are more profound reasons for doing this.

In Japanese culture, there is acknowledgement of the separation between inside and outside. By taking shoes off, we are taking a few moments to recognize this dichotomy. During these moments, we leave the problems of the outside world at the door in order to focus on the training in the dojo. When we put the shoes back on, we can leave the dojo and involve ourselves again with the outside world. In addition, young children were told that they could pick up evil spirits on the soles of their shoes. By taking their shoes off, they prevented the spirits from entering into the house. The toes of the shoes were pointed toward the outside of the house because if they did pick up any evil spirits, they would be led away from the interior of the home.

Walking on the Mat

First, never wear shoes on the mat. Additionally, before walking on the mat, it is customary to wait for permission from the senior instructor to do so. This is the case whether a student is on time or late. If a student is late to class, he/she should wait patiently at the edge of the mat. The chief instructor will give permission for him/her to enter. Once permission is given, bow to proceed onto the mat. If there is a line of students in class and you must walk across the mat, make sure to walk behind them toward the edge of the mat. Also try not to walk in between two people either talking or training; this is rude. Doing so is a distraction and interrupts what they are doing. Instead, walk behind them so as to not block their view. If you must, wait for them to acknowledge you, and then walk forward with a slight bow and your right hand extended as an apology for interrupting them.

Standing in Line

A commonly asked question by beginners is "How do we line up?" Before class begins, students should stand quietly on the mat and perform *mokuso,* or meditation, to mentally prepare for class. Everyone should be lined up in rank order waiting for the senior instructor to start the class. When the teacher enters, the senior student yells "Ki–o–tsuke," meaning "Attention!" This is soon followed by "Sensei–ni–rei," meaning to bow to the sensei. Class is now ready to start with the formal bowing procedures.

I have seen several different methods of lining up, depending on the individual dojo and the art being taught. In most schools, the senior instructor stands in front of the kamiza at the main focal point of the dojo, facing the students. The students are on the opposite side of the dojo called the *shimoza,* or lower seat.

There is some disagreement between schools because some schools differ regarding what side the senior student should line up on. In Aikido, if taking the students' perspective of facing the kamiza, it is common to have the senior student on the right and other students in descending rank order as we move left. However, other schools and different arts may have the senior student to the left. Although unsure, I speculate that this may be because in Japanese culture, the left side signifies life. The left side is also where the heart is in the body. Therefore, those who have had the longest life in the dojo would be furthest to the left. Since there are hundreds of different styles throughout the world, to say there is only one way would be arrogant. The important thing is that there is discipline and humility present.

The Uniform

Martial arts are military arts. Just as military officers wear uniforms, so should martial artists. Take pride in it. The uniform consists of a jacket and pants called a "*dogi*," or "gi" for short. There is also a cloth belt called an "*obi*" that is worn as an indicator of rank. How a person ties the belt is paramount and should be done carefully and neatly. Here is how to tie your obi.

First take one end of the belt and place it on the left hip with the rest of the belt placed in front of the waist

Next, wrap the belt around the waist two times

Then, take the free end and tuck it up behind the other layers of the belt and pull it through

Now, take the original end of the belt that we started with and pull it down, exposing it

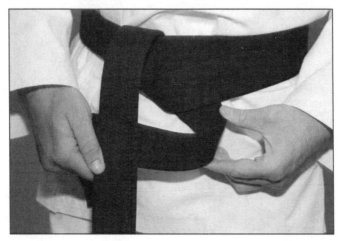

Make sure that the two ends of the belt are even and then cross the right end of the belt over the left end. This will create a loop

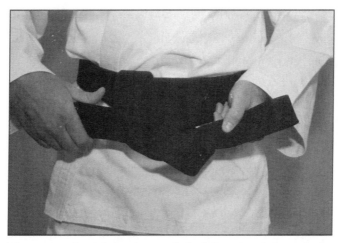

Next, wrap the right end around the left end and through the loop

Finally, pull the belt tight at both ends. This finishes how to tie an obi!

Traditionally, the gi is solid white, but I have seen some instructors wear black ones, which is fine as well. The pants should hang down to the middle of the ankle. When a person wears a colored, striped, or American flag gi, this is considered a non–traditional and inauthentic uniform used for "flashiness." When handling an obi it should never touch the ground, as this is a sign of disrespect. If the uniform and/or belt become undone during practice, it is proper etiquette to bow to your partner, turn around and face the wall, and then fix the gi.

The gi should be kept clean and ironed between each class because a clean gi represents a student's spirit. It is symbolic of the purity of mind one must have. For this reason, do not eat or drink while in uniform because of the high risk of getting a stain on it. Unfortunately, I have visited other schools where I have seen fruit punch and jelly stains on the gi of children. Do not stuff your sweaty uniform in a duffle bag after class and leave it there until next time. This is not only unsanitary but shows a lack of respect as well.

In some arts like Aikido, iaido, and others, the gi is worn along with a hakama. Hakama are black baggy pants that look like a skirt and also hang down to the ankles. The hakama have seven pleats, five in front and two in the back. Some believe that they represent the virtues of the samurai. The virtues are courage, benevolence, justice, courtesy, honesty, loyalty, and honor. However, the idea about pleats having virtues associated with them may have been added later as part of a modern speculation because I have found no written historical accounts of this being so. In agreement with David Lowry's book, *In the Dojo,* much of the martial arts have to do with practical applications, so it is more likely that this came about as a means to move more easily. The separation in the middle into two pant legs helps with sitting and getting up.

Long ago, not all Japanese wore hakama—only the samurai. This is because the samurai were considered of higher social standing than the merchant and farmer caste. The samurai wore hakama as a means to protect their clothing and legs from brush and tree branches as they rode on horseback. It was also believed that by wearing hakama, a warrior would hide his footwork from his opponent and therefore gain an advantage over him. Aesthetically, the hakama makes the fluid movements of Aikido look graceful and flowing, giving liquid beauty to the "art" aspect of the martial arts.

Interestingly, the white gi was originally considered underwear, and the hakama was the more formal dress worn over top. Morihei Ueshiba, the father of Aikido, required all students, regardless of rank, to wear hakama when they trained. It was not until later, due to the expense of fabric needed to make a hakama, that it was suggested that only black belts wear them. It is still a common practice in some systems to wear hakama only after receiving a black belt.

Part of the uniform etiquette is not only wearing and tying it, but also folding the gi and hakama. The uniform should be folded when a student enters the dojo, as well as before he leaves. True martial artists take pride in every aspect of dojo life, including the folding of the uniform. This goes back to the idea of shoshin. There are specifics on how this is done. Still, every school has slight variations. The following is one method of gi and hakama folding.

Start by laying the *uwagi,* or gi jacket, on the floor with the left panel above the right. Then fold the gi pants in half and place it in the middle of the jacket so that the top of the pants is in line with the inner seam.

fold in the sleeves toward the middle so that the outside seam is
straight and even

Grab the outer edge and fold it to the mid way point

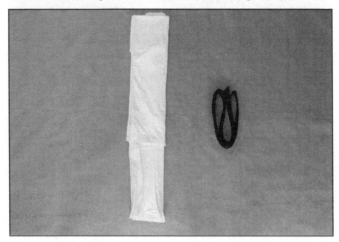

take the other side and fold it across to the opposite side

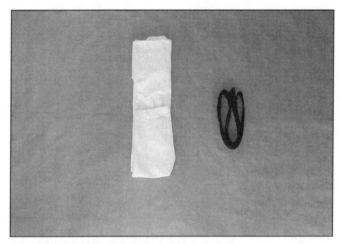

fold the bottom of the pant legs upward so that it is even with the bottom of the uwagi

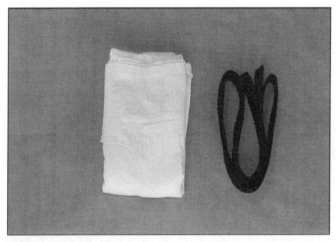

fold the bottom upward to the top

Once the gi is folded you can tie the obi around the gi as a student would wear it, or if you have a hakama, save the obi until the very end. Now, here are some photos demonstrating how to fold the hakama.

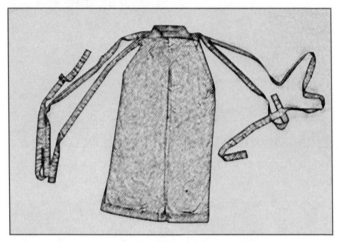

start by placing the hakam face down and straighten the pleats

hold your arm perpendicular to the hakama, a couple inches from the surface. Then grab the top and pull it, flipping the hakama over

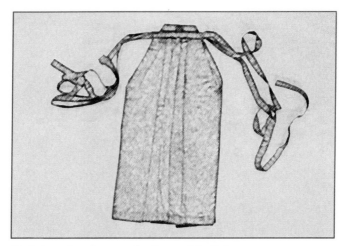

Straighten the pleats on the front of the hakama

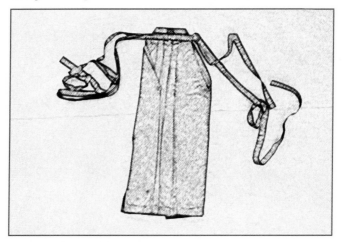

fold the left side of the hakama in so that the outer edge is even

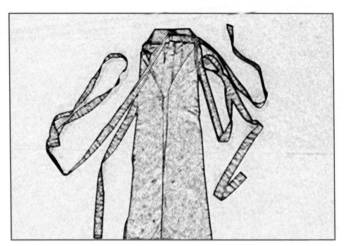

repeat the fold on the right side of the hakama

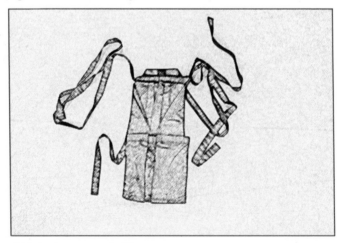

fold the bottom up half way

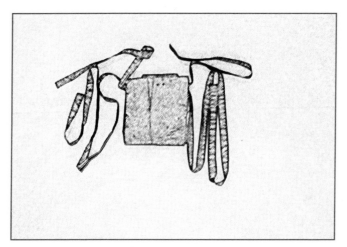

fold the bottom up to the top

next take the longer himo on the left and fold it into thirds

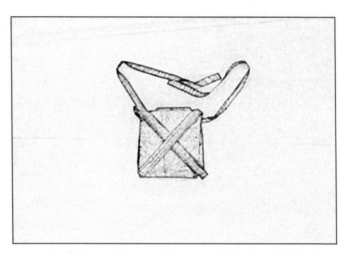

repeat the folding of the right himo into thirds then lay the himo diagonally across making an "x"

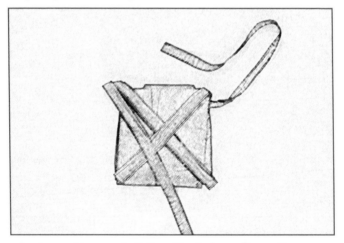

take shorter himo on the left and lay it down diagonally

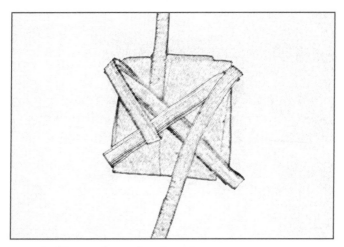

wrap the himo underneath and up the center

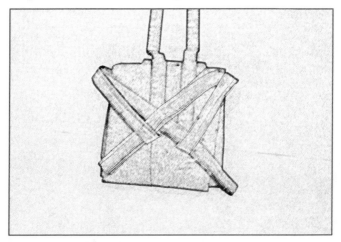

repeat on the other side

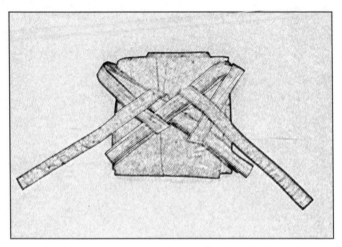

Fold the himo down again diagonally toward the side they originated

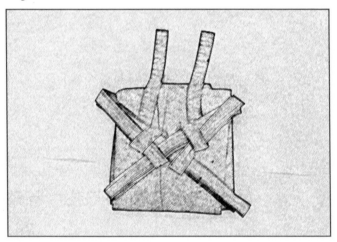

wrap the himo up underneath the top of the "x"

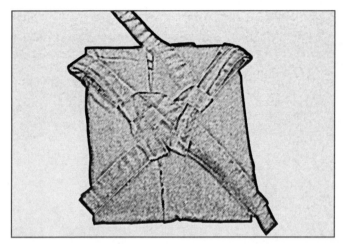

take the left side and go diagonally under the loop on the bottom right side of the "x"

Lastly, take the himo on the right side and go over then under the loop on the bottom left side of the "x"

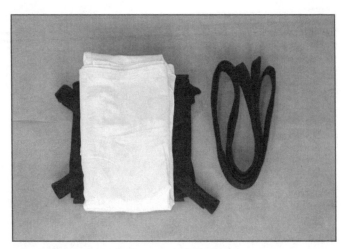

take the folded gi and place it on the hakama

tie the obi around the folded gi and the hakama like it was being worn by a person

Hygiene

For obvious reasons, good hygiene is necessary. Members should come to the dojo clean and showered. Fingernails and toenails should be trimmed, and hair should be cut or tied back. Also, do not drink alcohol before class, because besides exuding an odor that may be offensive, it also impairs control and judgment, risking safety.

A moist and/or a sweaty gi can easily grow mold and bacteria if left unchecked. By cleaning the uniform, the risk of spreading disease through blood and sweat on the gi is reduced. Keeping clean and tidy shows consideration for the others with whom you will come in contact during training. At the end of class, the mats should be swept and mopped clean to further prevent the spread of bacteria and disease. The process of cleaning the dojo can also be considered an act of *misogi* (ritual cleansing of the body, mind and spirit). Through the daily ritual of cleaning the dojo, we are also cleansing the spirit.

The Proper Way to Ask a Question

Before asking a question, make sure that it is pertinent to the technique that is being demonstrated at that time. Otherwise, wait until the sensei addresses that topic or the class ends before asking. It is rude and disruptive to yell out just to ask a question; therefore, students should follow proper procedures when doing so. First, bow to the instructor while saying, "Sensei, permission to ask a question?" Once the sensei gives permission with a "hai," the question may be asked. Following the answer, bow again to the sensei and respond with "Arigato, sensei," or "thank you."

Choosing a Partner

Many times during class, new students are unsure which person to choose to practice with. Generally speaking, there are several ways that are accepted. One way is when the sensei pairs students together. Sometimes it will be according to similar rank, but other times the sensei may have the higher–ranked students work with the newer ones. No matter how the sensei decides to pair the class up, accept it with a positive attitude because he probably has a good reason that comes from experience. Other times, the sensei will allow students to have the choice. When this opportunity arises, try to work with different people. In the street, students do not have the luxury of choosing who is going to attack them, so it is important that they work with as many different types of people as possible. This will increase overall skill, patience, and understanding of technique. When there are black belts training in the class, do not approach them to be their partner; it is more appropriate for black belts to select a partner to work with.

There are those students who display a poor attitude by sighing or making faces when they are paired up with a partner they do not like. It may be because of bad hygiene, they are a lower rank, or that they are too rough. Even in the best dojos there can be personal conflicts with another student. If this occurs, try to work it out in a constructive manner. If things stay unresolved, then speak to the sensei about working with someone else. If safety is the issue, make the sensei aware of the situation tactfully, and it will be addressed if necessary.

The other way that partners are determined is when a higher–ranked student approaches a lower–ranked one. It is not good etiquette for the opposite to occur. Although, a senior student should want to work with lower ranks as much as the higher–ranked ones because new students are more unpredictable and therefore keep you on your toes. On a deeper level, helping new members is a chance to give back to the dojo and perpetuate the art. It also gives the student a chance to work on the finer points of the beginner techniques that are the foundations of the art they are studying.

Dating in the Dojo

Since the dojo is on one level a social environment, it is only natural that some people find it as an opportunity to date another student. This is because when there is a common interest with such a positive message it is easy to develop bonds with others in the class, especially when spending so much time together. However, dating in the dojo is frowned upon and can become problematic. It can also cause distractions and all students need to stay alert to learn the lessons and avoid injury. The dojo is a place of spirituality and learning, so pursuing personal relationships removes the focus from the pure intent of the school. After all, a dojo is for training, not for lonely hearts. When students date within the dojo, it can affect the environment and the other students. How will members react if an argument develops between the two people dating? This has the potential to make everyone uncomfortable. Even worse, what happens if the two decide to break up? Often, when this happens, one or both decide to quit because the dojo then becomes a reminder of an unsuccessful relationship instead of a positive growing experience. Yes, there are exceptions when people meet and even get married because they met at the dojo, but the risks far outweigh the potential for a few successful romances. The dojo headmaster must look out for the best interest of the dojo and the majority of its members.

When students disregard any rules of conduct, they are disrespecting the sensei. If a student cannot restrain himself enough to follow this simple rule, how are they going to discipline themselves to learn and comprehend the more advanced principles and spiritual lessons of Aikido? Now, if a couple is already together before they join the dojo, then their relationship can be strengthened through their training. The difference is that a headmaster cannot, in good conscience break up an existing relationship when the couple is looking to reinforce it. If the time comes when it becomes disruptive, they may be asked to attend separate classes, keep their problems outside of the dojo, or eventually discontinue training all together.

Attending Seminars and Visiting Other Dojos

With the martial arts gaining momentum and mixed martial arts in the foreground, many students want to go to as many different seminars as possible. (A seminar is an event where martial arts instruction is available, which is different than watching a demonstration or expo at a mall or fair.) This is because many people feel that being exposed to more teachers will make them better martial artists.

Traditionally, this is not acceptable because a student is expected to commit to training with one teacher until he says otherwise. I know that many students are curious when they hear about the ability of another instructor or the effectiveness of another style, but it is more important for a student to concentrate on his own studies. If a person constantly feels the need to venture outside of his dojo, maybe he is in the wrong dojo in the first place and might want to consider finding a new instructor. The fact is that one cannot perfect their own techniques proficiently if he is also trying to learn everybody else's. By sticking with one teacher, students will be able to perfect those techniques without distraction. This is especially true since most students do not practice what they learned at the seminar after they attended one anyway.

Some may disagree and say that a sensei prevents his students from attending seminars out of fear that the student might learn more elsewhere and then decide to leave. On the contrary, restraint is expected to show loyalty and respect and is not done out of fear. If the student wants to leave, he will leave, and there is nothing that can be done to stop him. When teachers see that the student is committed to him instead of always looking elsewhere, he is more likely to give additional responsibilities to that student. To be safe and avoid being disrespectful, wait for the teacher to present opportunities for attending approved seminars. Almost all schools have them from time to time.

If a sensei wants his students to visit another dojo, he will let them know. When this happens, the next step is for the sensei to write a formal letter requesting permission for their student to attend. It is disrespectful to one's sensei as well as the sensei at the other school to just show up, so do not assume that the doors are always open. When attending a seminar or visiting another dojo a student should wear a white belt, no matter what his rank is, to show respect and humility while demonstrating a sincerity to learn from those he is visiting. Moreover, if a student is wearing an upper–level belt around his waist, people will expect that he can perform the techniques skillfully and participate in exercises that could be above their level of skill. If the student is not prepared, the situation could quickly become unsafe. Lastly, do not assume that just because a student was given permission once that they have an open invitation. The formalities are applicable each and every time.

Cleaning the Mat

After class, it is traditionally the job of the *kohai* (lowest–ranked student, usually the newest) to help clean the dojo. Just as privates in the military must perform menial tasks, so must the lower–ranked students in the dojo. The chief instructor of a dojo should not have to do any cleaning; instead, students should assist him or her by arriving early to class or staying late afterwards to complete it. This is not only a humbling experience, but a rite of passage. It teaches students, especially new ones, that they are part of a family—part of a whole. Eventually, after putting in their time, the job of the kohai will be passed down to the next new student.

Cleaning the dojo is not a punishment; students are preparing the space for the next group, which is simply an act of shoshin and courtesy. If it is done efficiently, it will only take a few minutes. In fact, many of my students look forward to this time as a way to transition from a rigorous class to the outside world. Cleaning with a positive outlook can teach us to take pride in everything that we do in life.

Here are some additional rules of conduct that are employed at my dojo. Feel free to incorporate as many as you like into your own training.

Do Not Enter Class Late:

Always wait for your instructor's acknowledgment. Remain outside the perimeter of the tatami (mat) until you are bowed into the class.

Ask Permission to Leave Class:

No one is permitted to leave the mat for any reason while it is in session. This includes black belts. Ask permission from the dojo headmaster first.

Do Not Talk in Class:

This includes black belts. Talking highly disrupts the headmaster's teaching ability and headmasters cannot teach if they cannot be heard. If you are talking, you are less likely to be focused on practice.

Only Perform the Technique Shown by the Headmaster:

No one is authorized to teach "variations" to a technique while a class is in session. (Variations will be shown by the headmaster if he wants them to be shown.) This disrupts training and has students and instructors doing techniques other than what the headmaster chooses. This impedes learning ability. Keep in mind that there is only one headmaster to a dojo.

Use Proper Titles When Addressing Black Belts:

Never use a black belt's first name in the dojo or at any martial arts function. This is very disrespectful. You may call them by their title—sensei, shihan, or soke.

- *No member shall display their techniques to a nonmember.* Why should others get to see these techniques so easily when you had to work hard to earn them? Techniques are for self–defense and defense of others only, not to prove your superiority or show off. Furthermore, you may not be qualified to teach and therefore an injury is likely to occur. This is especially true if the non–member has never studied martial arts or they have a physical condition that contraindicates this type of activity.

- *Do not show your ankles and the soles of your feet when seated.* In the Japanese culture, this is a sign of disrespect.

- *Do not lean on the walls*; it is a sign of laziness and disrespect.

受身

Ukemi: The Art of Falling

Ukemi, or the art of falling, is a profound endeavor in Aikido training and one with which many beginners have difficulty. Since we were children, we have been trying not to fall down. Even as adults, when we fall there can be a subconscious fear that others will laugh at us. Our instincts tell us that falling down will hurt, so why would being thrown down by another person in class be any easier? This is why ukemi is not only a physical practice, but actually has much more to do with conquering one's own fear.

Many students defeat themselves mentally even before they take their first fall. I have heard several students in my own dojo say, "There is no way that I can do that!" This is, of course, not true because eventually they all do. If we validate feelings of doubt and an inability to perform, failure is inevitable. Instead, ignore any negative thoughts and trust in the body's ability to perform as well as the falling methods that are taught during class.

We have all heard the phrase, "When you fall down in life, you have to pick yourself up and move on," hence falling is an exercise of letting go. It is a letting go of our ego and our fear and accepting our fate with trust in ourselves and others. Students initially feel a lack of control while taking ukemi and will therefore attempt to stop themselves mid–air to prevent landing harshly. All this does is disrupt the proper dynamics of a safe fall, and by over–thinking it, the risk of injury is increased. By fully committing to the movement in a relaxed manner, one is more likely to succeed.

If we can do this in class, can't we also start to apply these principles in our everyday lives? Whether a person is walking in the snow, carrying groceries, or roller–skating, ukemi is an important skill.

One winter when I was at college, I was returning to the dorm after shopping for groceries. I must have been carrying about six or seven bags when I suddenly hit a patch of ice. In a flash, I flew up in the air like a scene from *Home Alone*. Out of instinct, I threw my bags and executed a perfect break fall. Although my groceries needed to go to the emergency room, I walked away from the incident unscathed. As you can see, a person does not have to be in the dojo to benefit from knowing how to fall correctly.

In Aikido, falling is a symbiosis between *uke* (the person being thrown) and *nage* (the person performing the technique). In fact, there is a direct correlation between the amount of ukemi practice a student has and their ability to be a good nage. The more skilled an uke is at ukemi, the easier it is for nage to perform a technique safely. Conversely, if the nage (pronounced "nog ay") does not do his job well, then the uke (pronounced "oo kay") has a harder time taking the successful fall without injury. If the uke does not trust nage, the mind races, the body tenses, and the ability to perform a good ukemi become compromised. Also, by feeling what a technique is supposed to feel like when performed by a skilled martial artist, the uke can attempt to emulate those dynamics of the throw in their own practice. In fact, I have learned just as much about Aikido techniques by being thrown by my sensei as by watching them being demonstrated on someone else.

By constantly practicing ukemi, the mind and body become more relaxed, which conditions students to accept the challenges of Aikido training. I have also noticed that students who are skilled at falling are generally less anxious people outside of the dojo and can better cope with the stresses of everyday life. By using this mentality, we can strengthen our personal relationships, our jobs, and how we view the world. As in ukemi, we must trust in others not to hurt us and control our fears, or it may prevent us from reaching our goals. Respectively, by over thinking our life decisions, we can hinder ourselves from moving forward and becoming successful in other areas as well. If we get injured while taking ukemi, we still pick ourselves up and continue on. We must also do this in life.

There are several different methods of ukemi, with minor variations from school to school. I will explain them later, but do not attempt to perform these methods without a skilled teacher who can supervise and correct you.

Three Levels of Falling

For now, let's say that there are three levels of falling: beginner, intermediate, and advanced falling methods. The beginner level consists of the student performing basic falling techniques by themselves in order to learn the mechanics of ukemi and to get comfortable with being on the ground. The intermediate level consists of taking basic ukemi while being thrown by another person. The advanced level of ukemi includes taking high–impact break falls called *chugeri*. These are performed both alone and with a partner.

Basic Ukemi

Within this category, there are several different falls the student must learn. The first ukemi is *mae ukemi* (pronounced "my ookemee"), which translates into front break fall. When taking a front fall, you must place your elbows together in front of your chest while making a "V" with your forearms, palms away from you.

Next, turn your head to either side. This is important because if your head is not rotated, your face may hit the ground, which is never fun. Also, if your head is not turned, how can you see the attacker who threw you? If there is dust that was kicked up, there is a possibility of it going into your eyes. After rotating your head, allow yourself to fall forward like a tree that has just been cut down. Before the point of contact, you must exhale out of your mouth to prevent getting the wind knocked out of you. This is similar to sitting on a balloon if the knot is tied instead of opening the neck and letting the air out so the balloon can deflate without popping.

Upon impact, the forearms, from fingertips to elbow, should touch all at once. At the same time, kick out your legs and land on the balls of your feet. Remember to keep the stomach and knees from making contact.

Do not try to stop the fall by straightening your arms. This can send the force into the wrists and shoulders, causing injury

The second fall is *ushiro ukemi* (pronounced "oo she row ookemee") or rear break fall. Start out with your chin tucked down against your chest. This prevents you from banging your head against the floor and keeps you from getting whiplash. At the same time, extend your arms out in front of your body in a crossed position.

Next, raise your hands above your head and lower your body onto your rear. Right before the lower back makes contact, you must slap the floor with your arms totally extended and close to your feet. The reason for slapping is to disperse the force of impact on your body, so the harder you slap, the less shock your body will take.

The proper hand position is with your fingers together and slightly bent. The thumb is bent and cocked back. When you slap the floor, your hand approaches at a forty–five–degree angle, making contact on the ulnar side of the palm.

After you slap the floor with your hand, land on the balls of your feet with the heels up. Simultaneously elevate the stomach and hips, preventing them from touching the ground. This protects the low back.

The third fall is *yoko ukemi* (pronounced "yo ko ooke-mee"), or side break fall. This can be performed on the right or left side. For yoko ukemi, first extend one arm in front of you. This will be the side of the fall. The hand position is exactly the same for these falls as the other falls previously described. Place the other hand on your belt to simulate it being in use.

Secondly, bend the extended arm across your face and swing the same side leg across the body. Then lower yourself down by bending the knee of the leg that you are left standing on. The bending of the arm allows for more power in the slap, and the swinging of the leg exposes the hip for a proper side landing instead of landing on the low back.

The third step in yoko ukemi is to slap the floor and take the fall. After the slap, the legs must land properly. If it is a right side fall, the right hand is the slapping hand, and the right leg is fully extended with the ankle plantar flexed forward. The left leg is bent with the knee straight up, and the left foot on the ball behind the right knee. The right arm and right leg should be close to the side of the body and parallel to one another. When the legs do not land in this way, there is a high risk of banging a knee or the groin during the execution of the fall.

The fourth ukemi is *mae zempo kaiten* (pronounced "my zempo kai ten"), which translates to forward rotary roll. This fall can be done on both right and left sides as well. Start by making an arc with your arm. The fingertips should be together with palms face out. If the right foot is placed forward, then the right arm will be on top, and the roll will be done over the right shoulder.

Tuck your chin against your chest. Then place your hands on the floor on the inside of the forward foot. Use the upper elbow as a guide like a steering wheel. Wherever it points is the direction of the roll, so aim it straight ahead.

Finally, push off with both legs while keeping the arm from collapsing. Roll over the shoulder that correlates with the forward foot. In order to come out of the roll successfully, it helps to fold the back leg behind the forward knee.

The fifth ukemi is *ushiro zempo kaiten* (pronounced "oo she row ookemee"), or rear rotary roll. Start with your hands above your shoulders. Tuck your chin against your chest and lower yourself onto your rear as though you are going to do a backward summersault.

Next, kick one leg over the opposite shoulder. As you are coming out of the roll, plant the extended leg and use your hands to push up into a stance.

Intermediate Ukemi

When getting thrown, there is a natural tendency to tense up out of fear, or a feeling of lack of control, so continue to breathe, relax, and focus on performing the fall with proper technique. Do not try to hold on to the nage; this will compromise the fall.

As stated earlier in the "basic ukemi" section, there are times that we need a one–handed fall. Since the nage has the uke's arm, he will have to do a *yoko ukemi* (side fall). We will demonstrate this off of a *koshinage* (hip throw). As the uke is being drawn forward, he tucks his head down and bends the free arm across his face to prepare for the fall.

As the uke goes over, he will start to position his legs in the correct posture, which is one leg straight and the other leg bent with the foot behind the knee. Right before impact, slap the floor as described previously and exhale out of the mouth.

Advanced Ukemi

In advanced ukemi, there is an explosive nature that must be utilized without hesitation, drawing power from the floor as well as from the force of the throw. There are two types of advanced ukemi: *mae chugeri* (forward high break fall) and *yoko chugeri* (side high break fall). These are important in preventing injury for the more dynamic throws of Aikido.

First we will discuss Mae Chugeri. To begin, step forward with your right foot and bring your hands above your head in a crossed X position.

As you step forward, bend the knees to draw the necessary power needed to lift off the floor, and rotate over. The goal with this is not to bend your back, but instead propel your feet over your head while keeping the back straight. To obtain the proper rotation, snap the head and arms downward as you push off with the legs and feet. The body will rotate around a central horizontal axis, which, when performing this fall alone, will be the hips. When working with a partner, the axis is usually the arm of the person who is taking the fall.

Upon landing, the hands should make contact first to dissipate the force of impact. As the body continues to rotate out of the ukemi, the shoulder blades and the balls of the feet should make contact with the heels lifted off the floor. As in the ushiro ukemi, the stomach and low back is elevated. Make sure not to dive forward. Ideally, the head should land at the point between your feet before the ukemi began.

For yoko chigeri, begin the same way as the mae chigeri. The only difference between the two is that as the body rotates over, it will land in a side posture like the side fall (*yoko ukemi*).

With a partner, the person being thrown must learn how to feel the technique as it is being applied. By doing this, the uke can adjust in order to take a safe fall. Timing is also important. If the fall is executed too late then the technique will have been applied causing potential injury. If it is done too early, the landing may be awkward.

Let's look at how the yoko chigeri begins when the throw is chambered. At this time, face your own arm. This will be the axis to rotate around.

Use the momentum of the throw and push off with your legs to go straight over your head. Next slap with the free hand, and land in the side posture.

Good luck practicing ukemi. It can affect the rest of your training and your state of mind.

武器

Weapons and the Martial Arts

History

The study of weapons has been an integral part of the martial arts since their inception centuries ago. During the feudal time of the samurai, there was a push toward a separation of the classes. This dichotomy was created as a way to distinguish roles between the warrior caste and the farmers, artisans, and merchants. Because of this, there seems to be two different groupings of weapons within Japanese and Okinawan martial arts, one being the farm–implemented agricultural tools and the other being non–agricultural military weapons. This stratification of classes was reinforced by the confiscation of the commoners' weapons during the late 1500s. The removal of weapons from the commoners was done in an attempt to prevent them from pursuing any further uprisings against the emperor of Japan. Of course, in order to prevent being defenseless, the peasants of Okinawa adapted and began studying Chinese martial arts from the Chinese immigrants.

Over time, these arts started taking on an Okinawan distinctiveness, which evolved into the art of Okinawan te, or "Okinawan hand." Farmers also incorporated the use of farm tools as a means to further protect themselves. Interestingly, similar farm tools to the ones used by the Okinawans were found in China.

However, although there may have been some Chinese influence regarding the type of weapons used, the methods of their use as weapons were different. Eventually, these evolved weapon arts became integrated as part of the Okinawa Te and karate systems of the Ryukyu Islands and Japan. According to Mark Bishop's book *Zen Kobudo: Mysteries of Okinawan Weaponry and Te,* there are approximately fifty different weapons recorded, which include farm weapons such as the kama (sickle), Tonfa, or Tui–fa (which was the handle of a millstone), the Sai (a truncheon), and also the Nunchaku (wooden flail), which were originally used for the cultivation, harvesting, and polishing of rice. Conversely, the art of Kobu–jutsu was created on the mainland of Japan, and these are the ancient weapons systems of the samurai. The weapons of the samurai were developed purely for military purposes and include, but are not limited to, the sword, spear, and the bow and arrow.

Benefits of Weapons Training

Practicing weapons is an important part of martial arts training, even in the modern day. Besides any historical necessity to preserve these traditions or the fact that many weapon systems predated their empty hand descendants, the study of weapons can have great benefits. In fact, some of the movements found in various empty hand systems are originally derived from weapons arts such as the samurai sword. Also, many empty hand systems teach defenses against weapons as part of their curriculum. By understanding how to use a particular weapon, a student can better understand how to defend against it. Furthermore, although some would say that traditional weapons practice is irrelevant for the modern world, by training in these weapons one can easily apply the techniques to a household item like a cane, a broomstick, keys, or an umbrella and turn them into an effective weapon on the street.

Another benefit of this training is that through the practice of weapons, muscle strength and control are cultivated. Due to the added weight of the weapon and the need to make precise movements, those who embrace weapons practice often develop beyond those who dedicate themselves solely to empty–hand training alone.

Weapons are treated as extensions of the hands, and instead of viewing them as separate tools, a skilled martial artist incorporates the weapon into their natural movement. Actually, weapons practice can greatly improve empty hand technique. Those who pursue weapons training refine their posture, balance, footwork, and fluidity of movement. This is because in order to use a weapon effectively, one must learn to move the entire body as one unit, not as individual parts disjointed from each other.

This is especially difficult when using one–handed weapons such as the sai, the kama, and the tonfa. Unlike two–handed weapons like the *bo* (six–foot staff), the *jo* (four–foot staff), and the samurai sword, when using one–handed weapons both hands do not have the benefit of being connected through a single weapon. Instead, one must be aware of two separate weapons, and therefore two separate movements, simultaneously. However, both types of weapons practice provide a methodology for unified movement.

The way a person holds a weapon can make the difference between victory and defeat, so one of the first lessons a student learns is the importance of *kamae,* or proper guard positions. These are the initial ready postures that lay the foundations for executing a successful defense. By holding the weapon correctly, a person can keep an attacker from entering his space, and by doing so, create a fortified defense. The weapon must be gripped firmly, but not so tightly as to restrict movement. Conversely, if a kamae is executed poorly, it can expose him to being disarmed and even losing the battle.

To make the weapon part of us, we must constantly practice. Through constant repetition the movements become fluid and precise, and it takes approximately 10,000 repetitions of each movement with a weapon before beginning to integrate it into muscle memory. It is that repetition that also improves speed. This is one benefit of practicing kata. While the body integrates those movements into muscle memory, the mind also develops, creating synchronization between the two.

However, kata alone is not enough to become an expert in a particular weapon. Subsequently, spontaneous defenses must be practiced as well. By doing so, one can learn to react naturally with his weapon and be prepared to use it if and when a real situation arises. During practice, there is a potent psychological reaction that occurs when facing another person with a weapon. That reaction provides an intensity not often found in empty hand practice. It forces us to be extremely focused or risk being injured. Because of this, those who study spontaneous pragmatic weapons defenses often find dealing with an unarmed attacker to be far less intimidating.

Also, effective weapons technique has as much to do with power as it does speed. Movements must be precise with a powerful follow–through. For this reason, simply making contact with the target does not mean that the strike will be sufficient to incapacitate him. Just as ki extends from your fist when you punch, ki must extend through the weapon to have real power.

Additionally, through the use of weapons, a heightened sense of awareness and completely focused state of mind is fostered. By staying centered we reduce the risk of cutting ourselves or being disarmed. Skilled practitioners enter a state of *mushin* or "no–mindedness" in which the mind is totally empty and the weapon seems to have a life of its own. Interestingly, some samurai attributed this feeling to be help from the spirits of the elements that were believed to be imbued into their blade during the forging process.

Practitioners do not only become cognizant of themselves and their opponent but are also able to better perceive their relationship with their surroundings. Since a weapon has an increased length beyond a person's anatomical reach, the radius of his *ma–ai* (proper distance) will also be lengthened. Therefore, his awareness must also expand accordingly. The ability to judge distance is necessary to prevent damage to the weapon by hitting it on a wall or a tree, on the ground, or anything else in the way. Furthermore, by learning about judging ma–ai through weapons training, a person's ability for striking correctly with a weapon and also how to avoid both an armed or unarmed attack becomes honed. People who study weapons also develop a further understanding of different lines of attack and how to create retaliatory angles to subdue an attacker.

Weapons Training in Aikido

Morihei Ueshiba had studied many weapons styles throughout his life. His knowledge of weapons included several forms of *kenjutsu* (swordsmanship) like Yagyo–ryu and Kashima Shinto–ryu kenjutsu and also Hozoin so–jutsu (spear) to name a few. Ueshiba often said that Aikido is based on the movements of the sword, however; he transformed what he had studied and observed in other arts and made it distinctly part of Aikido. His application of Aikido movement and aiki concepts were infused into the weapons technique making them fluid and free flowing.

Aikido weapons training incorporates the use of wooden weapons including the bokken (wooden sword), the jo (four–foot staff), the tanto (wooden knife), and the hanbo (three–foot staff). In Aikido, weapons techniques are not considered separate from the empty hand ones. Rather, the weapons techniques are reflections of them. In fact, all empty–hand techniques can be translated into aiki–weapons training, whether it is with a bokken, jo, tanto, or hanbo. For this reason, all the aiki weapons are loosely similar in the way that they are used. Aikido weapons techniques are both beautiful and effective in practice while the ethical and moral teachings in Aiki–weapons teach that a strike or block can quickly flow into a sub-duel technique that provides a more compassionate ending than death.

Aiki–ken (the art of applying aiki principles to the sword) is derived from the samurai sword arts of iaijutsu and Kenjutsu. Just as in those arts, aiki–ken has a repertoire of cuts, blocks, and parries. Aiki–ken also incorporates throwing, pinning, and disarming techniques done in a manner consistent with other Aikido techniques. Aiki–jodo is the way of the four–foot staff. Although not as big or thick as its six–foot brother, the bo, it is both quick and powerful. In aiki–jodo, there is a repertoire of defenses that consists of jo–dori (paired practice), kata (forms), disarming techniques, locks, and throwing techniques. Aiki–jodo incorporates the same principles used in Aikido, so the movements are more circular in nature. The aiki–hanbo is a three–foot stick that is both a versatile and effective weapon. Similar to a nightstick, the techniques of the hanbo can be applied to an umbrella, a cane, or any stick around that size. Because of its smaller size, it is useful for close in combat.

Here are some of the other samurai weapons systems one can study:

Iaijutsu/Kenjutsu

The study of the samurai sword can be broken into two parts, and there are currently only a few samurai sword systems left that are taught in their entirety. The first part of sword training is Iaijustu, or "quick draw live blade sword art of war," and the second is Kenjutsu, or "sword art of war." The main difference is that Iaijutsu employs techniques from the sheathed position, whereas Kenjutsu is used once the sword is drawn. However, in order to truly understand the sword, it would make sense that a person studies both arts.

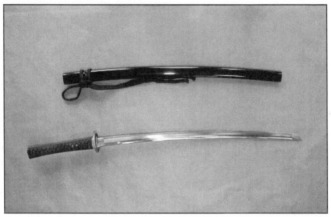

In Iaijutsu, students learn various methods of drawing the katana, and in some cases, the *wakizashi* (short sword). They also are taught how to cut from the sheathed position, proper methods of deblooding the blade, and how to quickly return the blade into the *saya* (scabbard). Commonly, Iaijutsu is practiced through kata, although paired practice with another swordsman is also part of training. Iaijutsu students use an *Iai–to* (drawing tool), which is a non–sharp metal blade that allows students to practice drawing with less risk of being cut. When using a weapon, like an iai–to, that is unsharp or even if it is made from wood, treat it as the real thing. Have respect for the weapon during practice and you are less likely to get injured when handling a real one. This means consciously not touching the bladed edges of a wooden *bokken* (wooden sword replica) even though the wood will not cut you. By training in this way, you are less likely to lose a finger when using the real thing.

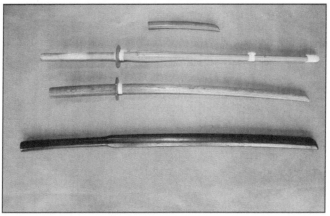

Weapons from top to bottom–Tanto, Shinai, Bokken and Suburi–to

Kenjutsu employs a wide variety of cuts, blocks, postures, evasions, and parries in order to subdue an attacker. There is also *tachi–dori,* which translates to "sword dance," and is the paired combat techniques. Kenjutsu exponents use bokken to safely train and *suburi–to* (cutting tool), which was designed to be heavier, to build strength and muscle control. Although I have seen both bokken and subri–to made from various types of wood like hickory, they are most commonly made from white oak for its durability.

Both sword systems incorporate an in–depth system of etiquette that adds to the mindset and spirituality of the sword; however, what differentiates these arts from

Iaido and Kendo is that Iaijutsu and Kenjutsu were more concerned with pragmatics on the battlefield and less with the spiritual nature often found in Iaido or Kendo.

Iaido/Kendo

Iaido is a traditional budo discipline focused on the drawing of the samurai sword. Unlike its predecessor Iaijutsu, Iaido concentrates on the "art" aspect of the sword. The goal is spiritual enlightenment, so this style aims at the perfection of self through the sword as opposed to victory on the battlefield. Most Iaido practice is done solo, with the sword starting and ending in the sheathed position, and kata is the vehicle for the *Iaido–ka* (practitioner of Iaido) to sharpen his or her skills. Visualization of a spontaneous attack during training keeps things fresh and exciting while developing technically correct movements.

Kendo literally translates to "the way of the sword." Some Kendo systems incorporate the use of Shinai (*bamboo swords*) and armor to train without injury, while others use bokken. The kendo armor is called *bogu,* which consists of various parts including the *men* (head piece), the *kote* (hand and wrist pads), the *do* (breastplate), and the *tare* (which protects the waist and upper legs).

Similarly to other Kenjutsu systems, there are kata performed between two kendo–ka that target different areas of the body while helping to develop fluidity. Another aspect of kendo is the competitive practice. In kendo, practitioners are restricted to certain targets, which is another way that it is different from Kenjutsu.

Bo–jutsu

Bo–jutsu is a combat method utilizing the six–foot staff and is an art of mainland Japan. This art is different and not to be confused with the kobudo methods of the Bo found in Okinawan karate. The weapon may be the same, but the methods of use are quite distinct. In Japanese Bo–jutsu, the techniques seem to be more power–based, whereas in the Okinawan bo, the techniques are designed for speed. This explains why the hand positioning is different. In Bo–jutsu, the six–foot staff was often used as a means to destroy a samurai's sword and is characterized through powerful strikes and effective blocking techniques. Practice is more concerned with effective blocking and striking as opposed to kata alone.

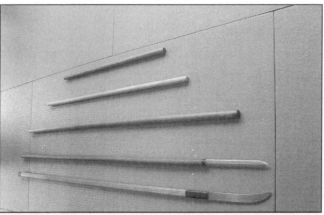

Weapons from top to bottom–Hanbo, Jo, Bo, Yari and Naginata

Jo–jutsu

The jo (four–foot staff) was mainly used against a swords-man because of its ability to easily deflect and even destroy a samurai's blade. In fact, due to the creation of this weapon, Muso Gonnosake was the only person attributed with defeating the famous samurai, Miyamoto Musashi.

As the story goes, Musashi allowed Gonnosake to live after defeating him the first time they fought, so Gunnosake left for a Shinto shrine where he prayed, per-formed purification rituals, and worked on refining his skills for several days. He then went on the road, study-ing other martial arts for years until he conceived of the idea to modify the jo's diameter and length to deliberately fend off another swordsman. Gunnosake also developed five jo techniques specifically designed to counter them. The second time he met Musashi, Gunnosake won. Out of respect for allowing him to live previously, Gunnosake returned the favor.

According to Donn Draeger's *Comprehensive Asian Fighting Arts,* the *So–hei* (warrior priests) of Kamakura times was among the first to systemize both Bo–jutsu and Jo–jutsu. Similar to the bo, the jo uses thrusts, parries, blocks, strikes, and disarms to subdue an aggressor.

Naginata–jutsu/Do

The naginata is a polearm between six and nine feet long with a curved blade attached to one end. The blade itself is about three feet long. At the other end was a metal cap that could be used for stabbing or thrusting. Of all the longer samurai weapons, this seems to be one of the most versatile because of its ability to block, strike, thrust, cut, and slash, allowing the user to utilize all parts of this weapon. Its long length was used to successfully keep another warrior at a distance, which is one reason this was a popular weapon with women of the time. It was also very successful against others on horseback, because it could easily dismount a rider or disable his horse. Unfortunately, there are very few systems of naginata currently left in existence.

Kyujutsu/Kyudo

Kyujutsu is the art of archery. Originally, Kyujutsu came from China and was used mostly for ceremonial purposes. When the art came to mainland Japan, its ceremonial functionality was maintained in addition to being used for hunting. According to Draeger, it was not until the martial unrest of the twelfth century that the bow and arrow became an important military weapon. Arrows were varied depending on strength, personal choice, and military rank. Arrowheads were also diverse in design according to their function. Common examples of arrowheads are the "turnip–head," the "bowel raker," and the "willow leaf."

Feudal Kyujutsu training required the archer to shoot a thousand arrows daily. After the introduction of firearms, Kyujutsu began to evolve into Kyudo, changing the use from a military weapon to a way of spiritual perfection. Kyudo is now an art form more than anything else.

*Here are a few of the Okinawan farm–implement weapons:

Kama

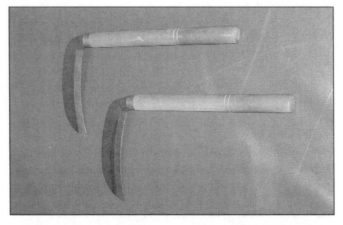

The kama is an agricultural tool used for the cutting down of rice. It is a hand–held curved sickle that was brought from China. This weapon has a wooden handle with a curved blade attached at the top perpendicular to the handle. The single edge of the blade is on the under side of the curve and is extremely sharp. A kama was used either singly or with one in each hand. It is a tool that can cut the body as it parries and can also hook, slash, skewer, and block.

Nunchaku

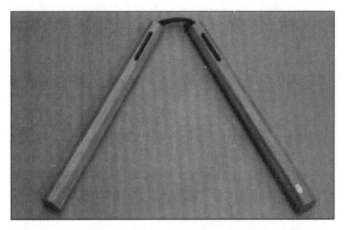

The nunchaku is a hardwood weapon that is popular even today. It has two wooden handles connected by a cord between consecutive ends. Although originally used as a flail for rice, it became an effective method of close–in combat. The nunchaku can be used to block, parry, strike, thrust, tie–up, crush, and throw an opponent. The handles can be of different shapes, including square, octagonal, or hexagonal and are connected with either rope or chain. Nunchaku techniques were utilized in conjunction with the principles of Okinawan te. Modern day use has changed from a purely combat intent to the more aesthetic demonstrations of sport karate.

Sai

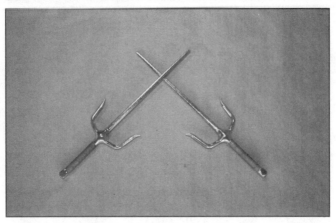

The sai is a solid metal truncheon utilized mainly by Okinawan systems, although its conception was much earlier, possibly from Indonesia. The length of the sai is approximately fifteen to twenty inches in length, and when held properly the tip should extend past the elbow. The weapon looks similar to a small pitchfork, with a main tapered shaft and a curved extension projecting on each side of the base.

Usually, when the sai were used, three were carried by the practitioner. One was held in each hand, and the third was kept in their belt. The purpose for the third was said to be because a skilled artist could pin an opponent's foot by throwing it into the ground. The sai was a proficient blocking weapon against the bo and bladed weapons. It could catch a weapon in its side projections or block with the main shaft. As retaliation, the sai could disarm, stab, or hit with the shaft and strike with the butt of the handle. There is a snapping–type action that is utilized to create power, which brings the sai from the cocked to the forward position.

Tonfa/Tui–fa

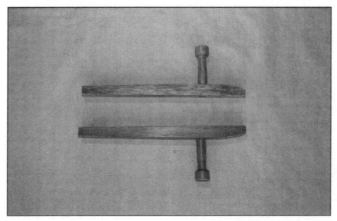

This weapon was initially a wooden handle for a millstone. The tonfa, otherwise known as a tui–fa, has a wooden shaft that lies along the forearm, similarly to the sai. There is a round handle that projects perpendicularly approximately five to six inches from one end. Commonly, two were used—one in each hand—and with a snap of arm, the tonfa can extend out so that the longer end can reach its target. The tonfa can block effectively and the strike with either the short or long end, depending on the distance and the specific target. Additionally, it is possible to punch with the weapon, allowing the user to achieve a lot of power as an extension of his fist.

Where and How to Choose a Weapon

Once you have decided to study a weapon, you may be wondering where to get one. There are a lot of suppliers available, whether locally or on the internet. Your sensei may also sell equipment, so check with him first. Do some investigating, but keep in mind when looking for a supplier that cheaper is not always better. This is especially true if you want something that is not going to break while blocking a full power strike. If you do not know what you are looking for, find a supplier that knows about that particular weapon and can give some pointers on what he or she has experienced. Also, remember that if you are buying from an overseas supplier then you will probably have increased shipping costs and long waiting times for the weapons to arrive.

When choosing a weapon, it is better to get one that will last. Ask your sensei if he or she has any criteria for what the weapons should be like. For wooden weapons, I recommend Japanese white oak because it seems to be the most durable. For a metal iai–to I recommend an aluminum–zinc alloy blade because it is light and well balanced, but for actual cutting with a sword, stainless steel is best.

Choosing the correct size of a weapon is dependant on the height of the user. When using a sword, the practitioner should grab the handle and choke up to the *tsuba* (hand guard). When the arm is fully extended at his side, the tip of the blade should barely graze the floor. Generally swords are about twenty–five to thirty inches in length. A jo is approximately four feet in length, but should go from the floor up to the person's armpit.

Once you have purchased a weapon, make sure that it is taken care of. Do not lean it against the wall because it can warp. It should be stored on a flat surface where the temperature is moderate. If the weapon is wooden, be careful of cracks or splinters. Try sanding it down to prevent others from being cut. Once the weapon is cracked it is time to replace it because it could break while blocking. *Ouch!* However, a quality weapon should last for years.

進化

The Evolution of
a Student

Just as every child grows and evolves during their life, so does an Aikido student. People have different outlooks as they grow from infancy to childhood, from being a teenager to being in their thirties, and going from the forties to becoming senior citizens. As a student begins his training, he is like a young child. Similar to life, each step in Aikido is cumulative, with each piece of information giving a more informed perspective of what was learned before.

A good analogy would be to compare training to a tunnel. A sensei has walked through the tunnel and come out the other side. He understands how long it is and what it takes to walk through it. A student, on the other hand, has just begun to walk through and has no idea of how long the tunnel may be. They must simply have faith that their sensei will guide them safely through. This can be frustrating to someone who needs concrete indicators of where they are along their training. Although, as I stated earlier, when the focus is on the journey instead of the destination, the training becomes more enjoyable without the need for constant reassurances.

Students start off trying to grasp basic movements and stumble along the way, but as they mature as martial artists they start to gain a better understanding of how things work. Eventually, if they continually train, they become seasoned aikido–ka whose skills are refined and who can perform the most complex movements effortlessly with grace and precision. However, the path to becoming a sensei is not an easy one. Aikido tests a person both mentally and physically, pushing him to constantly grow and redefine himself. It is through the tedious repetition of technique that a person's willpower and strength of character is challenged, stripping away stubbornness and ego until spiritual realizations occur. This is difficult to describe in words and may only be understood through personal experience.

During the journey, there are cyclical periods when we excel, times when we plateau, and even times when we feel like we are getting worse. To be successful, students must accept all of these as part of the learning process. Of course, it is easy to persevere during the times that we excel because we feel good about ourselves. However, it is during the plateaus and valleys—not the peaks—that a student can make leaps and bounds in their skill.

Unlike teenagers trying to grow up too fast and senior citizens wishing they were younger, Aikido students should forget about getting the next belt, technique, or whatever the reward may be for them because being in the moment is the best place to be. A child cannot ride a bike before they can walk, and an Aikido student cannot grasp advanced techniques before they comprehend the basic ones. When the time is right, the sensei will point the way toward the next step in their progression. When a student believes his technique is getting worse, this too is a "growing pain" that will pass if he can hold on and be patient. Do not let ego get in the way. Those who continue to practice will work through it and come out better for the experience.

Once an aikido–ka reaches an advanced level he may demonstrate *Takemusu–Aiki*. Takemusu–Aiki is the spontaneous execution of technique that emerges through the natural movement of ki. This state of unconscious movement manifests itself only after years of repetitive practice and is beyond knowing any one technique. It is the utilization of all techniques and concepts and allowing them to occur without thought, letting go of the outcome. Fast paced training like Aikido randori (defenses against multiple attackers) helps to develop Takemusu–Aiki. Those who achieve this level of skill are able to defend themselves in a confident and natural way, allowing the attack to determine the response.

As I stated earlier, when I began my training, I was one of the shortest children in my grade, weighing barely over 100 pounds. I was extremely introverted and had almost no confidence in myself. It was the martial arts that changed me into a confident, disciplined individual who is motivated and enjoys life. The question is, how did I get here? It is the journey that is the most important thing, and so we must ask ourselves: What are the experiences that help us grow? The truth is that all experiences help us grow, and it is this evolution that we should explore.

To understand the evolution of a student, I believed that it was more important for you to actually read about it from a student's perspective rather than from mine alone. Therefore, the following paragraphs are written by students. These students are from various walks of life and have been training from as little as a few months to almost eight years. Pay attention to their point of view as they describe their experiences. Also, notice why they started training, as well as how their personal philosophies evolved as their time studying Aikido increased. In addition, I want to state that I did not influence them as to what to write in any way, except for the instruction that it should be honest to the best of their ability. The students' excerpts will start from the least amount of experience to the most.

Richard Setyanto was a thirty–year–old male who had been training for seven months and had a white belt when he wrote this; here are his thoughts:

> I have been interested in martial arts since I was about eight to ten years old. Like every one else, I watched Bruce Lee, Jean Claude Van–Damme, Chuck Norris, and a few others. I have always been impressed by the speed, skill, and focus they were able to maintain. In the 1990s, Steven Seagal appeared on the scene. I didn't know what style it was, but it was way different from other martial arts. Being raised by a single mother did not allow for such activities.
>
> Moving on to February 2005, I realized I was really packing on the pounds. I was about 5'10" and 215 pounds on a small frame. I had already tried lifting weights, but it was just too boring for me to stick with and I didn't want to be built like a body builder. So when I saw an ad in the local newspaper for a martial arts school I knew it was time. I was a twenty–nine–year–old male trying a martial arts class for the first time.
>
> They invited me to come try a free private lesson, which was quite embarrassing on my end. I didn't last thirty minutes. It was supposed to be a one–hour intro/assessment of my physical condition. This was a turning point or wake–up call; it was definitely time to make a change in my life. After

realizing I was in very poor physical condition, I joined their school. The classes were composed of kickboxing, grappling, and general self–defense.

In the summer of 2005, I went to Sport's Fest to support people from my current school. (Sportsfest is a local event where hundreds of people come to compete and demonstrate in various sports such as basketball, hockey, arm wrestling, and martial arts.) Unlike other exhibitors at Sportsfest, David Nemeroff, Soke–dai was very personable and knowledgeable about several different types of martial arts. After talking to some people from other schools, I decided to try Aikido. My previous school focused more on belts and weight loss. Aikido focuses more on self–defense and mental exercises. The Aikido classes are based on the technical aspects of the art, not just the promotion from belt to belt. It is more martial arts, and less of an aerobic class.

I visited a couple of schools before I made my final decision. I visited a kickboxing school and a few other Aikido schools. Most of the instructors only wanted to know if I wanted to sign up. They wanted my money, not to help me. Also, they did not take the time to explain their classes and instructional styles. On one visit, I was ignored by the instructor and was not allowed to observe the class. I decided to go with Aikido Masters Self–Defense Academy because there was more emphasis on skill rather than weight and body fat. The personal attention made a big difference in my skill progression. I found that the footwork and some other movements for Aikido were difficult at first. The movements are controlled and closer to your opponent. There is more physical contact in Aikido. I also found it interesting that classes include self–defense maneuvers for armed assailants.

Aikido is a very different kind of physical training. After classes, I feel energized and centered. I look forward to my classes twice a week. My classes are a way to relieve stress and workout. If I miss a class, it affects my whole week. It is my outlet. I think Aikido has made me more confident. I know that I can protect myself. I am noticing that my overall physique is changing. I have noticed that my muscles are becoming more defined. In the seven months I have been doing Aikido, I think I am adapting rather well. Overall, I hope to continue training for many years to come.

At this point in his training, Richard was mainly focused on the physical aspects of training, which is common. As he had said, he began his training in order to get into shape and talks about the physicality of what he learned. It is not wrong to think this way; it's just one step in the evolution of a martial arts student. He is also correct in mentioning Aikido's ability to reduce stress and has made a positive realization that the martial arts are not about belts, but about skill. Richard has continued his training since writing this and his mentality is continuing to change for the better. Lastly, Richard gives a good message to other sensei out there: if you want perspective students to respect you, do not treat them like a burden.

Wade Bailey is another student, age thirty, who wrote this with ten months in Aikido. He started his training for a different reason, but like Richard, he was drawn to the many benefits of Aikido:

> In the year prior to initiating the study of Aikido, I had received an electrical injury that required rehabilitation. Having been restored to functional health, I was depressed and left with a persistent chronic pain and fatigue syndrome. Frustrated that any assisting medications generally had side effects that far outweighed the benefits, the feeling of depression and alienation from help grew stronger. This state produced challenges at work as well as at home.
>
> This may sound strange, but while watching one of the *Karate Kid* movies, I came to the conclusion that I was being controlled by my pain. What followed was almost utter defiance and determination that I would control it. I instantly knew that I required assistance in doing so, and I had formulated an association with martial arts training nearly twenty years prior. I recalled

the sense of discipline, structure, confidence, and achievement as the very elements I associated with those earlier years and felt a need for them in my life again.

I immediately began searching for a dojo to suit my needs in the Allentown area and decided to enroll as a student in the art of Aikido. To this very day, I am not certain what exactly inspired me about the dojo, but I do recall being quite impressed with the depth and discipline of all of the students. The first couple of classes I attended were quite overwhelming; not only was I concerned about performing techniques correctly and violating etiquette, but I was also introduced to the attention–grabbing joint locks and manipulations that allowed me to feel something other than my chronic pain. This experience was and still is an emotionally awakening experience for me.

It was not long before I realized how symbolic the relationship between Aikido's nage and uke represented a partnership that I desired as a model for relationships in my own life. This is not to say that I wished for more confrontation in my daily interactions but rather to discover more ways to cohesively work with others and develop a sharing of trust. One example of this is in regards to my work as a research chemist. The interpersonal relationships in such an environment can be extremely competitive and drive participants to exhibit destructive behaviors. In the dojo, Aikido practitioners take turns in each role of nage and uke learning together. Using this concept to attempt to develop more cooperative interactions in the workplace, I discovered that spending the time to understand other people's views and concerns on a fundamental level opened the opportunities for me to serve others' needs more successfully, develop trust with more coworkers, and made it easier to receive assistance from others. Without going into blinding detail, I also discovered that I felt a need for balance and sharing in the relationships I have with my wife and daughter. Simply recognizing that giving equal weight to hearing and being heard as important to maintaining solid rapport with my family became enough to relieve emotional burden and concerns about home life much the same as one might look at managing finances or even pain. Thus, the dojo became a place for me to contemplate and practice my interactions with the world.

Additionally, I learned some of the important Aikido principles regarding being connected with the ground or earth. In essence, I learned (probably more consciously than anything else) that my center (or hara) was not in my head but rather a number of inches below my navel. Simply acknowledging this and reminding myself that this is a scientific truth enabled me to more easily connect with the ground in order to help quench dizziness that constantly accompanies the pain I have been fighting. This, in effect, has made me aware of feeling the ground beneath my feet for the first time in my life. I put this to work and discovered how much more I enjoyed physical movement. Embracing these concepts has, much to the delight of my wife, helped to make me a better dancer (although still not a very good one) and even helped me to realize other "centers" that exist, such as those between two people.

After some time, I began to feel better even though the chronic pain remained unchanged. This was a reminder to me that some of the more important things to work on in one's life are not always those one would initially believe. In my case, pain management evolved from medical treatment to personal management of my emotional and physical state to the best of my abilities, and Aikido was leading the role in this change. This aided me in adjusting my initial attempts to control the chronic pain into simply not allowing it to have power over me.

Even though the learning of this valuable lesson began to relieve a considerable burden in my life, I was still challenged and frustrated that dizziness, nausea, and physical fatigue were present as a constant nuisance in everyday activities, especially while training in Aikido. I brought these concerns to David Nemeroff, Soke–dai, anticipating instruction on improving my movement techniques. Rather, I received an offer for therapeutic assistance in the form of craniosacral therapy, which I accepted. The therapy was not only very relaxing and opening to other areas of needed development, both physical and mental, but also served as an initiator for the important principle of increasing self–awareness.

In conjunction with the therapy, I received useful instruction and encouragement regarding meditation that I have found very important in being able to provide strength for myself and others when it is most needed. I have also found meditation useful in the challenging journey of connecting with my hara, or center. Though it may sound strange to some, among my favorite meditative actions are performing tenkans (body pivots) and cleaning the dojo's tatami (mats).

Even today the chronic pain remains unchanged, but I can certainly attest that it affects me considerably less than previously. I do not feel as controlled by the pain nor do I feel as strong an urge to fight it. This has given new breath to my desire for self–improvement, provided fresh and tangible reasons for continuing my training in Aikido as well as other arts, and inspired me to attempt adopting Aikido as a lifestyle for development and the search for life's joys. For this I give my respect to David Nemeroff, Soke–dai, his teachers, the late O–Sensei Morihei Ueshiba, and my fellow students.

In closing, I would like to point out that many of my friends, physicians, family, and colleagues express that they do not understand why I subject myself to Aikido training as it appears rough and unforgiving. They often joke with me about my training as being the visible actions of an early midlife crisis. Even if this turns out to be, as for the reasons outlined above, I cannot think of a more productive way to contemplate ones existence and find fulfillment in living. Regardless, I look forward to many more years of enlightenment through Aikido.

Wade's exploration of self–awareness reinforces the fact that Aikido is more than just a physical endeavor. Through Aikido he is gaining control of something that was spiraling downward rapidly—his life. It is great to see that with only ten months of training he is learning to manage a condition he has had difficulty with for years. His determination and commitment to improve himself is what moves him forward and what will continue to help him deal with his pain. Through Wade's realization of how important it is to give to others, he has been given in return a calmness of mind, a pride in himself and a better home and work life. His actions reinforce the idea of, "That which you put out will come back to you."

The next student is Mallory Zingone, who was a sixteen–year–old female with a little over a year of training:

My first class I was terrified. I was a short, teenage girl who was not physically fit or strong; on top of that, I did not know anyone else in the dojo. I remember I walked into the dojo and there was a class going on. Specifically I remember there were three or four guys all rolled up into a ball on the floor trying to choke each other while random feet and heads were sticking out like in the cartoons. For the first month or so, I was more out of my comfort zone than I had ever been in my life. I always felt so anxious before class, and then when I got there my movements were awkward and I felt very uncomfortable around the other guys. Gradually, I became more confident and comfortable doing techniques so I started going to more classes. Now after training for two hours a day, three days a week, the dojo has become my comfort zone.

My mindset has changed a lot since I started training. I had initially started to learn self–defense, but now I go because it is what I love to do. I have started to really like to learn new things and to meet new people. Which is not like me at all, I used to be really shy and scared of anything new.

I have learned so much over the past year and a half. I have learned how to take care of my body and myself. I have learned more techniques than I can count and there are many more on the way. I also learn about respect and etiquette.

Doing Aikido has definitely affected my life. It has given me a respect for myself and others that I never knew existed. For example, I used to reject men right off the bat. I thought men were the root of all evil, but now after spending so much time with them and training with them, I respect them and do not assume bad things about them right away. Aikido motivates me in other areas of my life. I actually want to do my homework, do well in school, and exercise, and eat healthy. I have changed a lot since I started training. I lost a lot of weight, became stronger, I have more control over my body and my mind now. In the beginning, I would try to wimp out on the hard things, but now I make myself do them and appreciate it afterwards. I am not afraid or intimidated by people anymore, well for the most part. My experience in the dojo is amazing because it is something different every day.

I think one of the best days that stick out in my mind was one night we were doing a ki exercise. We had to pick out an undisclosed person in the room who was told to think bad thoughts about us. I was so unsure of myself; I thought that I was not feeling anyone's energy, but then when I said who I thought it was, I chose the right person and that totally "rejuvenated my spirit." I always learn and feel new things during class, which is overwhelming sometimes but it is usually a lot of fun. Some other nights stick out in my mind as being extremely challenging. I would just work my body so hard that I felt like I cannot do any more throws, and then I looked at the clock and realized I had another forty–five minutes to go. Even though sometimes class is hard, it is very rewarding.

What is interesting about Mallory's thoughts is that after only a year of training, her total outlook has changed. One can see that when she started her training, the focus was about her physical weaknesses and insecurities. She felt out of shape, short, and not strong. However, as she continued, she became more confident and discusses having a healthier mindset and a drive that motivates her. She is now able to accept others without prejudging them and also has the understanding that there is a more to martial arts than just physical technique. Mallory has definitely made a life change that will guide her for years to come.

Benjamin Staples is an Aikido student at Aikido Masters Self–Defense Academy who wrote this after training for almost two years. Here is his personal evolution:

My experience with Aikido has been one mixed with physical as well as emotional challenges. I have to admit that when I first joined the dojo I was mostly interested in getting exercise. I was interested in losing some weight and, knowing that aerobic exercise accelerates weight loss, began to contemplate my options. I'm not a big fan of running, and my knees are pretty shot from years of downhill skiing so I crossed running off the list. I used to lift weights but I don't want to build a lot of muscle mass and I don't really dig the "weight lifting environment," if you know what I mean. I thought that Aikido would just be an interesting way to get in shape, and while it has certainly been that, it has also turned out to be something much more.

I spent my first months at the dojo trying to get as much exercise out of my training as possible. This approach had its advantages and disadvantages. Of course, one of the advantages was that I whipped myself into shape pretty quickly. I used my muscles as much as possible in each technique, ran whenever possible, and just generally welcomed anything strenuous regardless of the lesson being taught. I worked quite hard at making myself work hard. Defenses against multiple attackers seemed to consist mostly of football–style spin moves mixed in with some alpine slalom (downhill skiing) technique. I turned close–contact combat into wrestling matches, and my favorite part of class was the warm ups, where I basically worked myself up until I couldn't breathe and my face was blue. As you could imagine, this type of training didn't lend itself to improving my self–defense techniques but I didn't really care about that. I was interested in exercise. I lost about 10 or 15 pounds over the course of a few months and felt pretty good. I found it easier to get up in the morning, had more energy throughout the day, and slept better at night. All in all I'd say I was in pretty good shape. On the other hand, not focusing on Aikido meant that my classmates were progressing faster than I was. I started to feel a little behind my peers, and coming to class started to become a burden. I even went through a period where I thought I might quit. I mean, if I'm in it to get into shape and I've accomplished that, then why stay? Why not just walk a few days a week to maintain my weight? I don't think I ever really tried to answer those questions. The fact of the matter is that I did stay and it was the right decision for me.

I'm not sure exactly when it was, but several months into my training I started to focus on the Aikido instead of the exercise. You might say I began to view the techniques as an art form applied to combat rather than a vehicle for better fitness. I paid close attention to my instructor and tried to copy his movements. One interesting learning technique I developed was to picture myself in my instructor's shoes as he demonstrated a new technique. I would (and still do) sort of project myself into the self–defense position as my instructor walks through the counter–attack and it helps me remember each step. The point is that I started to concentrate on my Aikido training and I put a lot of effort into learning about the art.

A few months went by, and an interesting but wonderful thing happened. Several aspects of my training began to come into focus. Lessons that seemed trivial and uninteresting before had new meaning. Techniques I thought I had "licked" proved to be unmastered. I started to notice that I was wasting a lot of energy trying to execute moves that, with proper balance and concentration, could be executed without pouring all of my energy into them. I guess you could call it an epiphany. Whatever it was, it opened my eyes. I started to want to become better at Aikido and not just get into better shape. I attended class more frequently, looked forward to going to class, and enjoyed it more when I was there. This also had the unintended (but positive) consequence of getting to know my classmates much better and develop a respect for all they have accomplished. The whole transition seems like a breath of fresh air as I look back on it—something of a new awakening.

Taking an interest in my training meant that I started to learn all sorts of lessons that I had previously passed off as unimportant. In the past, I wasn't interested if it didn't involve me almost passing out from exhaustion. But I had become more focused and prepared, learning things that have turned out to be very helpful for me. Proper breathing is one example. I remember my first class when my instructor taught us to breathe properly. It was sort of a brief meditation class. I used to think that it didn't matter how I breathed, just that the air made it into my lungs. In fact, I thought, *The more air I could force down there, the better, right?* Then the instructions—in through the nose … out through the mouth … in through the nose … out through the mouth—slow deep breaths, concentrating steadily on the air flowing past my upper lip. We did this for several minutes while sitting still and I found it difficult to stay focused at first. I mean, how often do we really pay attention to our breathing throughout the course of the day? After a while though, I started feeling different. My muscles started to relax and my mind quieted. There was an overwhelming sense of calm—then—time lapse.

When we were finished, I remember looking at the clock and being a little startled at how much time passed. I felt extremely relaxed but not tired. My muscles were loose, and I didn't have to catch my breath even though I pushed myself quite hard for the last fifteen minutes of class. I just constantly concentrated on breathing in through my nose and out through my mouth over and over again. I was able to focus easier. It felt like I had better balance and less fatigue. I can't stress how important this lesson was to me. It is something that I've been able to apply to every aspect of my training. I find that I'm able to feel much more focused and relaxed even when the situation seems stressful.

Overall, Aikido has shown me how to persist when confronted with physical and psychological challenges. It has also given me a different perspective of patience and how it relates to learning. It has brought my attention to my own transformation and caused me to reflect on my progress not only in the dojo, but in other aspects of my life as well. Aikido has also given me a different perspective of what progress is. In general, I used to get quite discouraged when I didn't notice myself improving in anything I was trying to do. For example, there are times when I feel like I am not making any progress in the dojo. There are even instances when it seems like I am taking steps backward instead of forward. I have learned that these are important times in my development. These moments cause me to look at my technique objectively and recognize areas that need improvement. They also remind me that I am not the best judge of what I am doing right or wrong. I am not the expert, my instructor is. It may not feel like I am executing a technique correctly, but that doesn't mean that I am not. Conversely, just when I think I have something "licked," my instructor points out that my posture isn't correct, or my footwork needs improvement, or any one of several aspects of some particular technique that I thought I was doing correctly.

The same is true for my development as a musician (I am a percussionist). There have been several times when I thought my musical development had become stagnant. It seemed like progress had come to a halt when in actuality it was just part of the development process. It is much clearer to me now that I need to expand my timeline to notice progress. It's only when I look back at the last couple of years of my training that I feel like I've accomplished something. I've learned that whether it be Aikido, percussion, or developing software, as long as I make an effort, I am constantly getting better even if I don't notice it. In short, Aikido allows me to constantly grow as a human being.

Ben has made some important realizations, and so Aikido was the impetus for him to evolve. If physical conditioning is the only goal for a student, then I must reiterate his question: "Once that goal is achieved, what is the point of training?" Thankfully, Ben understood that there is much more and therefore began to grow. He also discovered that, as I stated earlier, we all go through periods of growth as well as periods that may seem like stagnation or failure, but they are really all periods of learning. Once Ben opened his mind to the idea that there was more to learn after he just looked without ego, his training became refreshing and exciting again.

Joshua Dasilva was a twenty–year–old who had studied Aikido for three years. This is his perspective of his evolution:

> My name is Joshua Santos Vieira da Silva, I am twenty years old, and I began to study Aikido as a sophomore in high school. Before I came to study Aikido, I studied several different martial arts including karate and Capoeira, but I never stuck with either of them for very long. To me, those arts were not challenging. I barely had to put any effort into my training in order to rise in rank. Also, because it was not challenging, I had no confidence in my ability to defend myself in the real world.
>
> I first became interested in Aikido through one of my friends at school. She started taking classes

and was very enthusiastic and excited about them. She made me interested through her energy and convinced me to go to a free class. At first I was very intimidated at all of the high break falls and rolls. I told myself that I would never be able to get my body to do that. However intimidating the falls might have been, I still had a lot of fun in class. Aikido, unlike the other marital arts I had trained in, actually challenged my body and mind. I felt like I was actually learning valuable information, and I had fun in the process. As for the high falling, I figured that I had some time to learn it before I was expected to be able to do it. So, after the first class I enrolled for classes and began taking Aikido and Aiki–jo on Thursdays.

As I progressed, I found that I was able to perform the techniques with ease, but I still found falling to be difficult. I found rolling to the left to be the most difficult and I was often unsuccessful. It discouraged me to the point where I began to entertain the idea of not coming to class anymore. If I did not go to class, then I would not have to deal with my rolling difficulty. I also felt that if I could not deal with the issue myself, then I simply could not do it. One day in class, I decided to pluck up my courage and ask the teacher about it. It took him all of ten seconds to correct the problem. I have not had trouble with rolling since then and have lost my fear of failing a roll. That day taught me a valuable lesson that I have carried on to the present day. When I encounter troubles in my life that I do not know how to deal with, I turn to someone who knows more than me for instruction. I choose not to run from the problem, but to seek help from someone wiser than I am that would know what to do. This skill has allowed me to traverse many things that could have developed into major life issues.

After getting over my fear of falling, I was able to truly focus on my training. As I learned more and more, I began to realize something. I was now in the possession of knowledge that would give me victory over my enemies, but how was I going to use that knowledge. If someone were to give me trouble, such as a bully, I had the ability to cause him serious damage. This would not only boost my confidence, but it would give me a respected reputation. When I hit this fork, I was forced to look back at the knowledge I had learned in class. Aikido teaches the way of the warrior, but it also teaches the way of peace. It had always seemed a contradiction to me that I was learning to defend myself and learning an art of peace at the same time. It was at this fork that I began to understand. I had the ability to solve my problems with force, but I was going to choose not to. I would not flaunt my ability in the face of my opponent or edge him toward violence, but

I was going to try to resolve the issue peacefully. If he were to physically attack me, then I would defend myself using what I have learned in class, but the art of Aikido itself is peaceful. An attack would be neutralized without serious harm to me or the attacker, and a potentially long and violent fight would be avoided. I also realized that it was my responsibility to keep the peace. My opponent does not know what I know, and is therefore, in a sense, younger than I am. It is my duty to try to resolve the issue, just as an older sibling would take responsibility over the younger sibling.

Recently, I have begun to see that not only does the philosophy of Aikido apply to combat techniques, but to all of life as well. I realized more and more how much life is circular and how Aikido mirrors that spherical nature. As I came to this realization, I also began to see that this has already been discovered by many different cultures around the world. Even the ancient Aztecs regarded the circle as sacred. This observation is very recent and I am still in the process of observing the circular nature of the world and its profound effects on our life.

The lessons and principles engrained in the art of Aikido has taught me much about the world around me, and will continue to teach me valuable lessons as long as I continue to follow along its path.

After years of practice, Joshua has touched upon some of the deeper lessons of budo. His commitment to training has led him to evolve spiritually as well. Initially, he was stuck on getting over his problems with rolling, but once he overcame his fear, his mind opened up to new ideas and experiences. As he grew, he realized the responsibility that comes with martial arts training and that if left unchecked, that knowledge can be abused. Joshua has also learned that part of understanding Aikido is showing compassion. Just because a person has the ability to send someone to the hospital does not mean that he necessarily has to do so. O–Sensei Morihei Ueshiba often emphasized this in his spiritual teachings. At this point in his training, his awareness has also expanded beyond himself and considered the interconnectedness of the world. Finally, Joshua has started exploring how the physical movements of Aikido technique are actually vehicles for more profound lessons that can be applied to all aspects of life.

Dodie Sable was a fifty–year–old woman who had been training over four years. She calls her story "Fear Cuts Deeper than Swords":

> I found my dojo on a fluke. There was a "Win a Free Week of Lessons" set up at a local Chinese restaurant. My husband and I filled out a card and put it in the fishbowl. Imagine my surprise when we were called and told we won! I was in my forties, and although in pretty good physical shape because I have a horse farm and also race endur-

ance with my horses, I had no martial arts background other than a year of tai chi when I was a kid. Everyone told me that I was too old to learn Aikido and I'd hate it after my week of free lessons was over. Boy, were they wrong. I was hooked from the first day. It not only got my adrenaline flowing and gave me the endorphin rush that I already have an addiction to, it put into perspective just how out of shape I truly was.

My husband lasted a year and quit. His leaving the dojo was partly because he felt that he was not accomplishing anything and partly because he was bored. Me? I kept right on attending training three times a week because it was great. The Aikido training I had been getting in the dojo has several applications in my life outside the dojo. There were several horseback riding incidents in which I felt I was not injured due to my training in falling properly. Also, the Aikido training taught me to move energies past me that were directed at me.

I also have a great love of the meditations and ki training. Both these practices have truly opened up my mind and made me more sensitive to those people around me. I have learned to be quiet in the face of a storm and be a willow, moving with the storm instead of fighting it. This has made me a better person, as well as given me strength to face a battle or to turn and walk away, and to know when to do either.

Aikido changed not just my physical lifestyle, but my mental lifestyle. Everything around me began to move in different paths from those I walked before Aikido. Remarkably, lots of people even noticed it, especially those people at my workplace.

Unfortunately, I began failing in my training in the dojo. I had reached a point at about twenty–eight months into my training where I felt I couldn't do the more advanced techniques. I didn't attribute this to anything more than I was not athletic enough to "get it" like the younger kids did. I could fall with the best of them, keep up a steady aerobic pace (even though I smoke) and most days I outlasted some of the younger kids in class. But I couldn't do the techniques. I would become rigid, forget how to move, forget how to transfer energy, and I got progressively worse.

The point of no return for me was a private lesson in which I started the testing for my orange belt rank, and I couldn't make the white belt techniques work during the test. I became so frustrated that during regular class after the private class, I broke into an emotional state of anger and tears and gave up. I sat out the rest of the class under the pretense of nausea and went home, vowing never to return.

I stopped the next day and spoke with Soke–dai because he had asked me to be a part of his demonstration at Sportsfest and I did not believe I could do the dojo justice. In fact, I firmly believed I would embarrass Soke–dai and myself, so I told him so. He listened quietly to my self–pity and self–degrading comments about my skills, and quietly told me that he needed me at the Sportsfest and I'd be fine. He never commented on my pity party or berated me for being childish, simply told me I was needed and it didn't matter to him whether I performed at peak or not. I still didn't feel very good about myself and I didn't have the heart to tell Soke–dai I was quitting the dojo after he told me that he needed me there. So I continued to come to training and practice for the demo at Sportsfest, vowing to quit afterwards.

In the meantime, Soke–dai found a new dojo. He announced the move and I thought, *Perfect! This is my opportunity to quit and have a reason other than I suck at Aikido.* The new dojo is located forty–five minutes from my house. I work a full–time job, run a full–time stable, and don't have a lot of extra time to do anything. That hour and a half of driving time could be well spent with my family, my horses, or my housework.

After the Sportsfest demo was over, I scheduled a private lesson. This lesson was really me telling Soke–dai "good–bye." The week before the lesson was to take place, Soke–dai approached me and asked when I was going to finish my test for my orange belt rank. I was flustered, because I didn't know what to say and he was pretty much telling me it was time to finish. He said we could finish it in the private lesson, and I kinda stuttered, hemmed and hawed and said, "Okay." Well, needless to say, I cancelled that private lesson. Even if I was going to stay with the dojo, I was nowhere near ready to finish the test and do the self–defense line. I couldn't even do the techniques in class without getting all tangled up on myself—how the heck was I going to stand in a self–defense line?

Soke–dai knew something was up, I'm sure of it. He asked me to be in the demo for his grand opening day. I couldn't think up one single excuse to say no. Once again, I came to training and practiced for the grand opening demo. During my practicing with Fulton, Sensei, I noticed that I was flowing techniques without thinking about it. I also was getting a lot of compliments on my Aikido from several upper–level students that hadn't been to class for a while due to college or injury. I wasn't sure why things were clicking for me, but they were. So we moved to the new dojo and the grand opening demo was a great success. I managed not to fall on my face while throwing my partner, which was a bonus. I had one month before my contract with the dojo needed to be renewed and I had decided to give it that time before I made a decision to quit. I also was being hounded by Soke–dai to finish my test, so I figured, if I made an ass out of myself at the self–defense line, that would be okay because I could quit anyway. I asked one of the students that I have a hard time working with to come and be my testing partner. I figured if I flubbed my test, I wouldn't have to stand the self–defense line. To my surprise, I actually did very well in the test, and only had two corrections to show Soke–dai afterwards. I found myself working with my partner instead of against him and the throws were working smoothly with little effort. At one point, I even asked the student if he was giving me the throws, and he assured me he wasn't. I was actually performing the techniques correctly.

By the end of the test, I was tired. I wanted to go home and soak in a hot bath. I decided since I was there, and home was forty–five minutes away, I should stay for the regular class. If I had known that Soke–dai would stand me in the self–defense line right away, I would have scurried away like a rat. I was barely able to get through the warm up without breathing hard and breaking a sweat—

I was that tired. When we finished warming up, Soke–dai announced that I was standing self–defense line that class and I almost fainted. Now, I got all stiff and panicky. I was not ready to stand the self–defense line; I had no confidence in my skills and ability to do self–defense. My God, I had just spent the last three months trying to figure out how to tell Soke–dai I was quitting because I couldn't do Aikido anymore. Although I know how to breathe and control my breathing, due to the training we receive, I was also fearful because I am older and all these students were twenty years younger than me. I also smoke, and that is a big draw back when trying to defend against multiple opponents.

When the line started, I completely forgot everything I learned and my mind went blank. I was so stiff and tight that I couldn't even move out of the way from the strikes. The second person to attack me hit me hard, in the solar plexus, knocking the wind right out of me. I couldn't get my air and Soke–dai stood on the sidelines and encouraged my attackers to keep coming. He said, "In the streets, they're not going to wait for you to get your air back. Relax. Move, breathe." All the while, the attackers are coming at me non–stop. Suddenly, my air came back and my body took over while my mind went blank. I was hurting from that blow, but was able to throw my attackers with little effort. On and on it went. Then I got hit again, very hard right on my breast, and it knocked me to my knees. I didn't want to get up and continue, and told Soke–dai I was done. He said, "No you're not. Get up." I argued that I couldn't breathe and he said, "Breathe later. Right now, defend yourself." And he told the attackers to keep coming. I just couldn't stand up. That blow really hurt and I couldn't see for the tears in my eyes. Here they come. I'm on my knees and they're attacking me. Believe it or not, I was able to defend myself from the seated position until I got myself back together.

The rest of the test I don't remember. I quit thinking and my body was running itself. I remember at one point during the grabs that I was losing my confidence after I had been tackled and pinned. I was struggling for air during a chokehold and told Soke–dai that I couldn't do anymore and he told me I could and I would and *move!* I did. I managed to get my fingers to a nerve point and my attacker released me. Whew. And on and on it went. For hours it seemed.

When Soke–dai said it was done, I was so tired I could barely lift my arms. Soke–dai put the students back in line and told me I had to push myself across the dojo on my belly and knuckles to finish the test. *What?* He said when I had reached the other side that was when I would pass the testing. Oh my god, I didn't have the strength to stand, let alone push myself across the mat. The students all started encouraging me, giving me kudos as I dragged myself over the mat toward the finish line.

When I reached the other side, Soke–dai congratulated me on standing self–defense line for twenty–eight minutes (felt like three hours), and the entire dojo cheered for me. That was very heartwarming. Needless to say, I was very sore for two days afterwards, and my entire breast was black and blue and green and yellow for almost a month. And once that was over, I found that my Aikido became better, more flowing and my techniques were working perfectly well. Seems that once I got past that which frightened me (the self–defense line) I was able to relax and perform as my training taught me. So what I learned from that was that "fear cuts deeper than swords," and if I ignore the fear, the sword won't hit as hard.

It is okay that Dodie had doubts about herself, her ability to perform, and whether or not she was going to quit. The point is that for whatever reason, she worked through it. I knew she was having these doubts even though she did not mention them to me, but I also knew she had to deal with them on her own if she was going to be successful at overcoming them. By going through her valley of difficulties, she was able to evolve, which she has. There are times when she still has issues to tackle, as does everyone, but I believe that the way in which she approaches them has changed for the better. Since her test, her Aikido has continued to improve, and she has elevated her status as one of the senior ranking members of the dojo. In fact, she is currently running her own children's program at a local community college in addition to teaching regular classes at my dojo. It just goes to show you that no matter what your age, if you have the proper attitude, you can accomplish almost anything.

When a person progresses in Aikido from a student to a sensei, it is an exciting time. They have taken a step forward that few people have the determination to achieve. It is interesting to watch that transformation and the change in perspective that happens from it. Nicolas Fulton, sensei, is one of those people who made it after much hard work. He started training with me in my children's program and has continued up through the ranks as an adult. For this reason, I have not only seen him change from student to sensei, but from a child to a man. Here is what he wrote:

> As a child growing up in the United States, I was raised in a culture constantly watching and adoring the martial arts. The Power Rangers, Teenage Mutant Turtles and movies like the *Three Ninjas* and *The Karate Kid* were some of my personal favorites. There was something about being able

to fight and fight well that had a strange allure to it. I am quite sure I was not the only kid in America who, after watching a half hour of the Power Rangers, was forced to go around the house spinning, kicking, and punching invisible mutant bad guys. Hence the draw of summertime martial arts programs and the YMCA karate club were certainly appealing. From about the ages of seven to eleven, I tried different summer camps and kung fu lessons and felt an attraction to some of the arts, but never a deep interest because I never felt it was the real thing. I always saw the same routine at the schools; either it was what appeared to me to be an impractical Kung Fu Eagle Scratch technique or a karate class that had bullies as the black belts who promised to give me my black–belt rank on my second day if I could answer some irrelevant trivia question. Moreover, in every school I went to, they seemed only to be kicking and punching, which became tedious to me after the third or fourth class. Where were those amazing stunts that the Power Rangers did all the time, the flips and spins and secret techniques that I had seen in those martial arts movies? The only fruitful experience I can remember about this time period was my introduction to meditation in my kung fu class, which at least gave me my first look into the world of internal energy. So the martial arts remained at this time in my viewpoint, mostly as a silly pastime. I was a big kid and was sure that I could win a fight against any one of these silly little kids who broke pine boards with their hands. Thankfully, I never really had that thought challenged because I could have been sorely wrong.

There are sometimes events, which take place in people's lives that inevitably change them forever. The one that affected me the most to this day was my first day at Nemeroff, Soke–dai's dojo. I was about twelve years old at the time, and my best friend, who was also my neighbor, and I decided to try out an Aikido lesson at the dojo where his younger brother had been studying for about a year. I went in with him, not expecting any more than what I had seen at the last martial arts classes and camps I had attended, but I shortly realized that this art named Aikido was much different than anything I had seen before.

I had the distinct impression after my first class that I was going to like this art. We were not just drilling kicks and punches, but actually learning how to fall and how to roll and how to throw someone to the ground! I found this very exciting, as did my neighbor, and because we would both be doing it together, we decided to sign up and see how things would go. I must say that I had never before been one for sticking to a program for very long. I would do something till I got tired of it and then I would call it quits. This same day, though, on the drive home from the dojo, my mother asked me, "So you liked it?" and "Do you think you will stick with it and get your black belt some day?" to which I replied, "Yes, I think I will."

I started to then take more than just the Aikido class at Nemeroff, Soke–dai's dojo. I went to the Goshinjutsu class, the Aiki–jo class, and the Iaijutsu/Kenjutsu Sword classes. I seemed to like the weapons classes in particular and for some reason had a natural affinity for the Japanese katana. I really started to enjoy these martial arts classes; they seemed so in depth and practical that I knew I was learning the real thing. What's more, I was learning under a master who had real skill. I had seen martial artists before, but my teacher's skill, stamina, knowledge in the arts, and technical strength always intrigued me. Moreover, there was always a purpose to why the samurai would have used these certain techniques, which always fascinated me as well. There was more to these classes then punching and kicking to the beat of the headmasters chant. So I continued training and learning.

Also there was this strange concept of "ki" that kept me intrigued as well. It seemed to be this amazing force that was supposed to be properly utilized in the martial arts to make techniques more powerful, or amazing things like seeing Soke–dai take kicks to the groin painlessly. I was not sure exactly what it was or if I believed in it at this point, but I started meditating every once in awhile and realized that even if I did not feel much (or what I thought I was supposed to be feeling) it was at least relaxing.

I realized after about six months that I started to feel a bit competitive. It seemed to me that older students seemed to understand what they were doing before I did, that they could put the techniques to work while I was still fumbling around with my feet. I attributed this feeling to going through puberty, with growth spurts and all that comes along with it, although now, looking back, I realize that I was not very coordinated at the time either. I also realized that I had never needed such coordination as I did while practicing the martial arts. Yet one day, after I had learned and sufficiently grasped the techniques for my yellow belt in Aikido, I had my first test, which was an unforgettable stepping stone in my training.

I was about thirteen years old and was matched up against one of, if not the highest ranking student in the class, with whom I was supposed to demonstrate my self–defense techniques. I was frightened but I also felt good about what I knew, and after the test was over, I shall never forget hearing the Soke–dai's words: "You've passed," and how much that meant to me. I wanted to thank everyone and everything in sight, seeing as I had wanted rank for so long and finally got it, but then I realized that, besides the instruction I was given, it was my own hard work that got me my yellow belt and I felt good that I was capable of earning what I did.

I realized that the martial arts were not about the number of techniques or how fast you learned them, because they are a long–term process and a long–term commitment. Training itself should not be a competition! This is where I discovered that the uphill progression in the martial arts is not a diagonal slope up, but more of a slightly sloping staircase, which is to say that there are high points of progress in training, and then there are periods which may feel like an eternity of non–progression. I have learned throughout the years though, that the progression always comes. Sticking to this theory has kept me going through my most challenging times.

I continued on with the arts throughout high school and the more I studied them, the more they became a part of me. The way I walked changed. I had better posture. I had a more positive image of myself and would prefer to resolve problems as soon as they presented themselves, instead of letting tension gather. I was physically fit and found out that even though I had never practiced the sports in my gym class, the physical and mental elements of sports were not very different from those of the arts, and so I excelled in gym class. My mind was calmer through meditation practice and I was able to focus sharper and longer than before allowing me to excel in my academic studies and in my field of foreign languages.

Along with all these changes came a healthy self–esteem that allowed me to be proud of my accomplishments. But just like in the arts, if I grew careless in being proud, I would get a sharp strike back to reality. I was (am) also the only person in my entire group of friends to never have used illegal drugs. This sometimes made it hard for us to get together if I knew they would do things that I was not going to do; but in the end, when they realized that they did not need drugs to be as happy as I was, they looked up to me as an example. That was a wonderful thing to hear, even if it was years later.

In high school, I became interested in the Japanese language and got to go to Japan for a month during the summer after graduating from high school. This was one of the most wonderful months of my life and in learning Japanese and going to Japanese schools, I was also able to partake in the martial arts clubs offered by the schools there. I very soon found out that the Japanese were quick to judge foreigners who say that they have studied Japanese arts in the West, due to so much fraud in Western martial arts schools claiming to teach authentic Japanese Ryu's. Yet to my unending delight, my training proved itself tenfold in the Japanese martial arts clubs. There in Japan I had the opportunity to practice kyudo, judo, and kendo. Kyudo was completely new to me and I was terrible! But in judo I found myself to be formidable and was able to throw and pin almost all my opponents due to my jujutsu training. They actually said I would go too hard and I ended up scaring many of the students because my jujutsu techniques were so much rougher and non sport– like. In those moments, as all other times, I was proud of my school in Pennsylvania.

In the kendo club as well, I realized that it was much different than the kenjutsu that I study back at home, but once again I discovered that kendo was tailored to be a sport and was not necessarily the most effective way to wield a Japanese samurai sword. In practicing with the class, I was given a dummy to strike with the shinai (bamboo sword) and then later an armored opponent because they were shocked to see that I could properly use a shinai. Then while holding my sword at the ready on my side, the sensei came up to me and asked, "How do you know to hold your thumb over the tsuba like that?" to which I replied, "I have been studying the Japanese arts of Kenjutsu and

Iaijutsu for five years now in the United States," I had told him this before though; he must have disregarded what I had said, in disbelief that my ryu in the USA could be authentic. Yet now he was staring at my hand hold in astonishment and then he looked me straight in the eyes and said, "You must have a very skilled and wise master," to which I replied with all the humbleness I could gather in my proud response, "I agree, sensei, thank you very much." I was thereafter awarded the bamboo sword I had used as a gift and souvenir of my kendo classes at their school. I came back home with two such bamboo sword souvenirs and a handbook to high school judo, along with a scroll in calligraphy that reads, "Aikido."

After I got back from Japan, I started to realize just how closely woven together the martial arts are with meditation and I firmly believe that self–defense without meditation only comprises half of the martial arts. Along with meditation comes deeper understanding of oneself, improved coordination, increased power and a sense of control over oneself and thus one's environment. Some theories that I have been developing within myself and am putting into practice with my martial arts due to my meditation are those of stillness and one mindedness. I believe that stillness describes one who is perfectly prepared and who exhibits an efficiency of technique. If being struck at, it is best to stay still, calm and ready to move at just the last possible moment to get the most out of the technique. In dodging a blade the best time to move is the last possible moment, hence making it that much harder for your opponent to evade your reaction. One–mindedness describes the harmony and unity of the body and the mind enabling the body to react just as quickly as the mind. Thus if the body acts as an extension of the mind, there is no wasted time in reacting to outside stimulus in the manner with which the mind has been trained. Hence oneness is achieved and the practitioner can defend himself in an extremely efficient manner.

Later, I had the opportunity to study intensively because I had no job after being out of the country for most of the summer. I was at the dojo almost every day, and by the end of the summer, I had passed my shodan test in Aikido and my Iaijutsu and Kenjutsu Okuden tests. I also was granted the title of sensei and then went from being just a student to being a student and a teacher of the martial arts. The following year I started at a university in Canada and soon started my own Aikido classes at the university's gym. When I started to teach, I officially became a dojo headmaster, and to this day my dojo's name is Endless Horizons Fukasa–Kai. The Dali Lama once said that the only way to learn something completely is by teaching it,

and this I found out right away with students asking questions on techniques and wanting to know
how to defend themselves in different scenarios. I
also learned much more about the finer points of
the arts just by watching my students start their
own path in the martial arts.

I did have one student in particular who reminded
me of myself when I felt competitive with my
neighbor near the beginning of my training. He
would always try to stand out in class somehow
and would boast of his past experience in the martial arts and wondered how I could be so much
better and have my own school if we were of
almost the same age. I never said that I was better
than he was but he was in my dojo studying my
arts, so I was in charge.

One day, though, he finally challenged me in front
of the whole class because he did not like the classical techniques we were practicing in class and
doubted my arts actual effectiveness. So because
it was the end I told this bold student to wait one
moment as I bid everyone else adieu until the
next class, then I asked them to please close the
doors of the basketball court on their way out.
My student was set on teaching me a lesson in the
martial arts, and so I told him that if he wanted
to spar with me, I would not hold back. We stood
at either end of the circle in the middle of the
court, bowed and then I let him come at me. He

gave me a barrage of "nothing strikes" meant to fake me out, and without having to block most of them, I stepped in and gave him a smart tap on the face, just enough to jar him and get his nose to bleed a bit. Then he came at me again, angrier and more determined. I stepped to the side and gave him a swift kick to the stomach, which he did not expect because we had never worked kicks in class. He thought I did not know how to do them and consequently he tumbled to the ground and started to cry. He got up then and decided to come at me with flying kicks which I simply evaded, and in the end he lost his own composure (due likely to his anger) as he did his balance, and fell on his side weeping. I helped him up and he begged my forgiveness and told me how he realized that he had a lot to learn, and from that day on, he was my very best and most loyal student.

As an instructor of the martial arts, I realize that I have a lot more to learn. I am still a student in every sense of the word. In teaching the arts, I learn just what it is that I need to keep vigilant on and in what I need more training or practice. Despite all the hard work and responsibility of being a martial arts sensei, its rewards make it worth the difficult path. In teaching people techniques that can save their lives or even just help them to feel more confident about themselves I find all the reward in the world. I still have students writing me to thank me again for things such as meditation techniques that have helped them relieve stress during exam periods, and if that is all that they have utilized the martial arts for then so much the better!

In conclusion, I have realized over these years that the path of the martial artist is a very long and profound one; so much so that I will be able to keep following it for the rest of my life, to keep improving myself through constant practice and meditation till I either become perfect or die along the way! This is another quixotic lesson in the arts. We all know that perfection in all aspects is unattainable, but what better way to occupy the time in one's life than by striving to continually improve oneself mentally and physically in order to be a full, vibrant and helpful person? This to me is a valiant goal and worthy undertaking.

Lastly, David George is my oldest student with eight years of training under his belt when he wrote this. He is not only a dedicated student but has now become an instructor who has opened up a school of his own. He continues to study with me regularly because he knows the journey never ends. With over four years of teaching experience, a new evolution is beginning for him. This transformation is one that a teacher goes through as he grows from a beginner instructor into an advanced one. Although he is just starting this journey, he has shown the spirit of someone far along this path. This is his perspective.

I suppose I was pre–disposed to training in the martial arts ... well, at least as much as anyone that remembers watching Kung fu Theatre on Sunday afternoons. I was always awed by the way the men and women in these motion pictures seemed to "float" and move with such power and speed. But of course, at that time I was a youngster wrapped up in baseball, wrestling, and other "traditional" sports. Then, during the mid–eighties, I was again inspired by Hollywood martial arts, this time by none other than Steven Seagal, who demonstrated a very powerful and at this point unknown (to me) martial art. I would later discover this art to be Aikido. But even though awe–struck by his ability to handle multiple attackers and effortless looking throws ... I still did not look into training in any of the martial arts.

So what was the catalyst that finally got me to visit a local dojo almost a decade later? Well, there were actually two main reasons. The first—one of my employees began showing me a few basic wrist locks (I later discovered these were nikkyo and sankyo) that he had learned a few years back in an Aikido school. This simple demonstration sparked my interest once again. The second—I was going through some turmoil in my life, and I knew I wanted a physical outlet to help deal with the daily stresses of life, be it a weight lifting gym, fitness club, a hobby of some sort—so with a friend suggesting I visit a dojo only fifteen to twenty minutes from my home (at the time), I ventured to Aikido Masters Self–Defense Academy.

The first thoughts I had—I knew I needed to commit to this ... to commit to training for at least six months before deciding if this was something I was going to pursue for many years. I knew this from the other sports I had partaken of over the years. I was never a truly gifted athlete ... I always had to work hard to excel, and I wanted to give this new venture its fair time and effort. I also knew I had to get past the trepidation of being older ... would there be mostly 16 year old kids with relentless energy and a lack of empathy to an older beginner. I remember images of "black belts" in my head ... all with the technical ability of a true master. Surprisingly, besides the head instructor, as I scanned the dojo training room for the first time I noticed that most of the students were either yellow or white belts. I must admit, while still somewhat cautious of the "higher" ranked students for the first few weeks, I was definitely a bit more relaxed seeing that I wasn't alone in my beginner's quest to train in a martial art. And, to my pleasant surprise, my fellow classmates showed compassion and understanding, using the appropriate amount of force to perform their techniques.

I had some other concerns that I remember soon after joining the dojo. Would I be able to handle the various falls (ukemi) that I was being instructed to perform. It seemed like these students of Aikido and Jujutsu could fall and fall with untiring energy. Would I get hurt? Was a high breakfall really possible? I saw my fellow (but senior) classmates performing these stunts (as I then perceived them), but could I? Should I? With this one must truly begin to trust in himself, his teacher and mostly in his inner ability. Also, saho (etiquette and respect) was something new to me. While in wrestling and other sports there's a certain respect for one's coach, teammates and competitors, in the Aikido dojo there is much, much more to learn, understand, and appreciate about respect for one's instructor, fellow classmates, of the dojo and training area, and so on. At times even this seemed a bit overwhelming. What was appropriate, what wasn't, and when?

Injuries, injuries, injuries. Now this is something I can painfully remember (and still deal with to this day). In the beginning, I can remember blindly pushing myself to continue training even with twisted ankles, sore wrists and so on. Now, I'm not saying you shouldn't continue to train with some injuries, but listen to your body. If your wrist is sore, don't do kotegaeshi (wrist twist); do something else. Today, after training for an hour or two, I have two almost constantly inflamed shoulders ... so, I train hard, but when my shoulders start to "speak" to me I lighten up. This isn't getting soft; this is listening to your body and training intelligently.

Balancing your training with your needs, goals and the many other aspects of your life is also very important. I can't stress enough keeping balance in your life. Besides injuries that may limit your training, I've found that you must also listen to your inner voice in regards to balancing your training for proper health and wellness. If you make a martial art a part of your life, which, it may well become, make sure you balance your training and study with your personal relationships and obligations as well. Make sure you include your wife or husband, children, and friends by inviting them to demonstrations and special events. These demonstrations are a great way to educate your loved ones, as well as the general public, on the power and grace that is Aikido, and, more personally, why you train in this wonderful art. This is your opportunity to share the unique principles and ideals of non–violence in a self–defense martial art. Remember, a good martial artist knows that all positive aspects of his life are equally important.

With this being said, as I instruct various training classes in the dojo I have noticed one constant variable: consistent and repetitive training in the dojo equals improved technique and mental focus. It is imperative that one attend classes on a regular basis to learn and revisit the numerous physical techniques and mental disciplines of Aikido. If one is patient with himself, reasonable with their goals, and trains consistently in the dojo, he will begin to understand the fundamentals of Aikido, and will begin to enjoy all aspects of the training. Even today when I hit a plateau, road block, or even outright mountain, be it a difficult technique or lack of mental focus, it is revisiting these "stumbling blocks" in the dojo with my teacher and/or classmates when I can see the light at the end of the tunnel. The path of Aikido training is never ending. There is no destination, only an enjoyable journey.

Martial arts training can be extremely fulfilling, even enhancing your life. It provides you with a physical outlet, mental focus, even spiritual awareness if you want or allow it. Martial arts and Aikido in particular can provide you with a lifetime of enjoyment, from the technical aspect to the ability to use Aikido to avoid stress and chaos from the "outside" world. Morihei Ueshiba, founder and creator of Aikido, was quoted as saying, "Aikido is not an art to fight with or defeat an enemy. It is a way in which to harmonize all people into one family. Aikido is the principle of nonresistance. Because it is not resistant, it is victorious from the beginning. Those with evil intentions or contentious thoughts are instantly vanquished. True budo (Aikido) is invincible since it contends nothing. In true budo there are no enemies. True budo is a function of love. Love protects and nourishes life. Without love nothing can be accomplished. Aikido is a manifestation of love." I use to think that I fully understood what Ueshiba was saying…but after many years of training and now instructing I am humble enough to recognize the deeper truth in the above words. As the saying goes "for Aikido a lifetime is not long enough to learn all there is to know." May your quest and journey in the martial arts bring you as much fulfillment as it has brought me.

It is the sincerity of practice and the pursuit of knowledge that moves a martial artist forward—not a piece of fabric or the number of techniques in their arsenal. In order to go from one stage of our evolution to the next, there must be patience because time is a key component to becoming a skilled martial artist. Change is happening all the time. There are no shortcuts to becoming a master, only hours of hard work. Those who train with passion will progress faster than those who simply go through the motions, and since both are at the dojo anyway, they might as well work toward mastery instead of mediocrity.

From reading these students' stories, you can begin to see that as a student delves further into Aikido they receive benefits far beyond physical skill. Aikido training fosters positive attitudes and warrior's spirit, eventually laying the foundations for a better way of life. The evolution of an aikido–ka never ends as long as his or her training continues. Continue to evolve.

Section II
Training the Mind

The Myth and Mystery of Ki

Martial artists, scientific researchers, and therapeutic body workers are just a few groups of people who address the idea of universal energy. Depending on the culture, group or system, the theory of energy has many different names. The Chinese call it *chi* or *qi* (pronounced "chee"), the Indians of Middle Eastern descent call it *prana,* and the Japanese refer to it as *ki.* Each one may apply it in different contexts, but it is all the same thing. Internal martial arts like Aiki–jujutsu and Aikido derive their power and efficacy from ki instead of muscle strength or brute force, but what is ki?

Universal Energy

Ki (pronounced "key") is most easily defined as "universal energy," or "internal energy," but understanding the concept of ki is sometimes difficult. It is considered the animating force of the universe and the thread that connects all life. In truth, since ki is beyond the scope of the mind, it is indefinable. However, in order to start comprehending what it is, one must delve into rigorous practice and experience it firsthand. This is because the theory of ki is a profound concept that is beyond words. It is infinite in nature.

Even though we cannot see it with our own eyes, we can all agree that energy exists. Without energy we could not power our cars, our computers, or just about everything we use in our daily lives. We can also acknowledge as scientific fact that there are bioelectrical currents that run through the human body. These currents help transmit nerve impulses and messages to the brain in order to maintain its normal healthy functioning. Without these currents, the body would cease to work and would therefore die. Just as an electrical circuit functions better when the connections and the current are strong, the same is true of ki in the body.

In traditional Chinese medicine (TCM), there is a basic underlying philosophy of the body that energy travels along energy pathways called "meridians." These meridians are directly connected to the different organ systems of the body. When there is an imbalance in the natural flow of energy through the meridians or in the organs themselves, the outcome is a tangible dysfunction. The resulting dysfunctions can be anything from back pain to cancer, depending on the severity of the imbalance. Acupuncture is one method in which a TCM doctor can address these imbalances and correct the flow of internal energy. Some other methods include qigong ("chee–gung"), yoga, internal martial arts, and other styles of meditation. As the flow of ki is strengthened, the better our immunity, our energy levels, mental focus, and the ability to cope with stress will be. (Later on in this chapter I will demonstrate some exercises that you can practice at home to help develop ki on your own.)

People's recent opinions on ki greatly run the gamut from believing that it does not exist at all to believing that it is some kind of mystical magic power. The latter is partially due to the seemingly amazing feats people claim they can do, including people taking full strikes to the throat and groin without injury, breaking a spear with the neck, or decreasing a patients' pain and/or health conditions in one or two sessions of acupuncture or some other ki–based therapy. Although initially I was skeptical, I have seen ki in action firsthand far too often to discredit its existence. Nevertheless, it is up to the individual to do the work and make the decision if and how ki practice can be incorporated into his or her life.

One day I was able to convey the existence of ki to a gentleman without even trying. I belong to a business networking group that allows its members to explain what is done at our businesses in order to help each other promote them. When it was my turn, I decided a demonstration would be much more effective than simply giving a speech or slide show. It sure was! I started off demonstrating the art of Aikido by having an assistant attack me. Quickly, I pinned him on the floor in an arm bar, making him unable to move. I then transitioned into a demonstration of my other business, which is doing craniosacral therapy (For more information, you can go to "http://www.upledger.com" *www.upledger.com* or www.therapy-4healing.com).

My volunteer was complaining from low back and neck pain, so once he was on the massage table, I began to address his issues while explaining what I was feeling as part of the therapy. Do not worry, his neck and back pain was not from my arm bar. After I finished, one of the other members of the group approached me, and what he said really surprised me. He said, "Boy, your demonstration was awesome, but frankly I was a little intimidated."

"Oh, by the Aikido?" I replied.

Now this is the funny part: he said, "No, by the therapy!"

When I asked him what intimidated him, he told me that he had never seen someone connect so completely to another person through touch and it was much more than what he had ever seen in a massage. He continued by saying that since he is very guarded both emotionally and physically, and knowing that my volunteer was the same way, it was scary for him to see me read the body with such ease. That connection I made with my patient was in part by perceiving and understanding ki. To put him at ease, I explained humorously that doing this type of work will not make him tell me his deep dark secrets. Instead, I told him, I am only there to help my patients in a non–invasive way, free from judgment, in order to provide them with some relief. As we parted, he smiled and said to me, "You see the world differently than everyone else here, don't you?"

Breathing and Ki

Understand that ki not only has to do with our energy, but our breath as well. The adult lungs hold approximately eight to ten pints of air. Most people breathe while only using a fraction of that capacity. This means that a large percentage of air is stagnant in the lungs. By learning how to control the breath, which is one thing that ki practice does, we maximize lung capacity and therefore increase the amount of oxygen in our body significantly. This results in more energy and improved health. Although this is only one step in the process, by controlling the breath, the ki is improved.

I know that a lot of people do not believe in the existence of internal energy and the many benefits it can offer, but it is important to consider a few things before totally discrediting its efficacy. Firstly, I want to state that ki is not a cult or religion, nor does it conflict with any religious beliefs. In fact, there are many religions that discuss meditation and controlling the breath. If breathing conflicts with your personal beliefs, you may want to reconsider them. Besides, one of my qigong teachers, Brother Bernard Seif, is a Salesian Catholic monk. If he does not have a problem with ki conflicting with his religion it most likely will not conflict with yours.

Ki practice unifies the physical, mental, and energetic systems of the body. Even Western systems like biofeedback use breath control to relax the mind in order to reduce pain. This is just another way to tap into the healing power of ki. Whether you believe in the Western ideas of medicine or older Eastern traditions, know that they do not invalidate each other; actually they are complementary philosophies of a larger picture. Just think, if you wanted to travel to New Jersey, there are several different routes to get there. Choosing one route over the other does not mean that you will not end up at New Jersey; it is just a different path to your destination. The same is true of both Eastern and Western concepts of the body.

Dr. Kenneth Choquette, an osteopath and western medicine pain–management specialist and owner of Pennsylvania Pain Management in Allentown, Pennsylvania, writes:

> Evaluating and treating chronic pain patients for many years has provided me with insights into the complexity of human health. The presentation of symptoms isn't always accompanied with anatomic or even physiologic explanations.

Response to treatment does not always confirm what we thought we knew about the body and how it works.

These unexplained functional features can be better understood if we underscore our known physiology with the knowledge of an Internal Energy or "ki." This non–palpable power runs through all beings and ties us back to nature. We are not separate beings but part of this family that is bound by forces that can be the only explanation for the integration of our existence and for the underlying functionality of our bodies and lives.

Meditation is one of the ways that we can try to better understand and eventually harness that energy that fuels our existence. It is also exponentially beneficial in regards to relaxation and stress reduction while providing us with a channel to better utilize ki. Meditation has been proven to lower blood pressure, lower heart rate and reduce symptoms of anxiety and depression whereas medications needed for treatment have been significantly reduced or discontinued. Gastrointestinal difficulties have been helped as well as improving the sense of well–being.

The contribution of "Eastern medicine" thinking and knowledge while understanding its philosophy helps compliment standard western medical practices to better afford us a more complete appreciation of how we function and what can be done to maintain and improve health. To ignore eastern medical practices and not to include its knowledge base into daily practical medical thinking is to cheat our patients of the best and most comprehensive medical treatment available.

To help prove the validity of ki, several researchers have made efforts to measure and record it. Through the use of infrared and kurlean photography (photography of energy fields) they have been able to photograph our energy fields, and certain low voltage measuring devices have confirmed that the body's energy seems to follow along the path of meridians. As stated in Kenneth Cohen's book *Qigong, The Art and Science of Chinese Energy Healing,* one study done by the Shanghai Institute of Hypertension, a division of the Shanghai Second Medical University, talks about the correlation between ki cultivating practices (like qigong) and improved health. In this thirty–year study, the survival rate of the chi–practicing group was almost double of the non–practicing group. Also the incidence of having a stroke and death due to stroke in the non–practicing group was approximately double of practicing group. "When forty of the patients were diagnosed by ultrasound, the qigong group were found to have stronger heart muscles and better left ventricular function."

Benefits of Developing Ki

No matter what walk of life a person comes from, developing ki can benefit them. However, before someone can reap the rewards from ki practice, it is important to have confidence and trust that it will work. This is not a placebo effect, but the mind controls the body. If the mind does not want to accept the idea that vital energy is within and around us, the body can be resistant to receive the benefits. The mind can also direct ki, so ki is therefore limited by the resistant mind.

One of the advantages of ki training is that it increases overall energy levels. Obviously, if the body is able to draw in more healthy energy, you will feel less fatigue. Just like recharging the battery on a computer keeps the hardware running, replenishing the body's energetic systems will allow it to function more efficiently. Think of ki practice as the body's daily necessary battery recharge.

In Eastern medicine, there is a belief that when our pre–natal ki, which is the energy we are born with, is depleted by illness or by the activities of simply living out our natural life, our bodies will die. This is also why it is valuable to practice methods that strengthen and replenish our energy. Similarly, ki practice will help improve the immune system. Like the computer, frequent tune–ups mean fewer breakdowns of its major systems. When our body's systems, like digestion, do not have to struggle to function, it can allocate more of its energy to fight disease. All in all, if our energy is weak, any and all of our bodies systems can break down and result in further dysfunction.

Some people equate the feeling of healthy ki to an adrenaline rush. Although harnessing ki taps into the body's inner strength and cultivates a greater overall awareness of ourselves and our surroundings, it is different than the rush experienced from a boost of adrenaline. When a person feels adrenaline, the body becomes excited, the heart beats faster, and the mind races losing control. By developing ki, the mind and body become calm, creating a clear mind and the ability to produce an efficient action.

By practicing in various ki methods, people's emotional states can often be stabilized. Those who commit to practicing regularly often achieve a calmness that allows them to better cope with their emotions and the external stresses of life, because on several levels, they are more balanced. The more a person practices and harmonizes with the energy of the universe, the closer to his true nature, and therefore to happiness, he will be. This may be because by becoming more in tune with the ki, our body also develops a stronger connection with everything else around us.

When we go against our true nature, the lessons of life seem to get harder. This commonly feels like bad luck. One of my sensei, Jose Andrade, would always ask me, "Are you happy?" Usually I would answer "Yes," but I would also tell him of various issues going on in my life at the time. In response he would say to me, "David, life should be a vacation." In hindsight, I think he was telling me to appreciate everything around me and do the things in life that are in line with my true nature instead of resisting them. If we hate our jobs, our spouses, and our lifestyle, it creates undue stress in our lives and therefore disrupts the flow of ki in our body.

I am not saying that anyone should necessarily give up there job and leave their spouse, but by working on ways to improve ourselves and our environment, we can come closer to attaining a more positive existence. It is complacency that creates stagnation, and it is not until we take responsibility for our own actions that we can move forward toward a better life. Since learning how to control our breath can directly affect physiological and psychological states of being, it is the first step in taking control of our lives.

Aikido and Ki

There is no Aikido without ki, and in fact, Aikido literally translates to the way of life in harmony with ki. Aikido is often referred to as moving Zen or a form of meditation in motion because a state of *mushin* can be achieved during practice. As a result, Aikido is also a practice of developing the ki. An aikido–ka unifies his energy with that of the attacker, creating a blending between the two. This is called *ki–musubi,* or the tying of energies. By doing so, the aikido–ka eliminates resistance and is therefore able to allow the attacker to subdue himself. In Aikido, students are taught to extend ki. What this really means is to project our energy and visualize with our minds in order to follow through with set goals while harmonizing with the world around us. The extension of ki should be happening all of the time and is not something to be turned on and off. When we are attacked, it is not enough that our energy is flowing well; we must blend with the force of the attack. It is a culmination of timing, calmness of mind, and the unification of nage and uke. When done properly, the aggressor is thrown to the floor effortlessly in what may seem as almost unbelievable ease. If we stop short and do not follow through with our action, it will not succeed. To extend ki, we must see past what is immediately in front of us, and visualize our intent.

In some martial arts there is something called a *kiai* (focused yell). A kiai is the harnessing of ki into a vocal projection. This is seen most commonly in striking arts like karate, but can be used to create extra power in a throw as well. By giving a kiai, our energy and spirit are concentrated into a forceful yell that can focus the mind to follow through our intended action as well as startle and imbalance the attacker.

Ki–developing methods like *mokuso,* or meditation, should also be practiced regularly in order for a person to receive a greater benefit. Many say that a minimum of fifteen minutes is needed to bring about therapeutic change in the body, but to be truly effective more time is needed. More time dedicated to practice will lead to more profound results. I recommend at least a half an hour a day of practice to start, increasing the duration as you progress. Some people find it difficult to quiet the mind during mokuso with thoughts of their families, their jobs or tasks of the day seeping in. When this happens, acknowledge the thoughts and then let them go without dwelling on them. Then, return to emptying the mind.

Interestingly, by practicing with other people simultaneously, there is an exponential increase in the amount of ki. This effect could be similar to the harmonics of a tuning fork where when one is put near another, they start to resonate similar frequencies that amplify one another. Also, there is no such thing as too much of this type of work.

How to Breathe Correctly

I realize that everybody can breathe, but there are various methods that help to maximize respiratory function. One method is called abdominal breathing, or diaphragmatic breathing. Many athletes, martial artists, and singers use diaphragmatic breathing in order to utilize their total lung capacity, improving oxygen intake.

Start by breathing deeply in through the nose and out through the mouth. Breathing should be performed as slowly as possible, with each breath flowing smoothly and continuously from inhalation to exhalation. As the inhalation begins, fill the lower abdomen with air, gradually moving upward, until the breath completes at the diaphragm. When exhaling, start at the diaphragm and continue to deflate the abdomen until the air is totally expelled. The visualization of the exhalation should end at the *hara*, which is at the bottom of the abdominal cavity approximately four inches below the navel.

A helpful idea is to picture a glass of water. As water is poured into a glass, it fills from the bottom up. As water is emptied from a glass, it is removed from the top, downward. Picture the breathe moving in the same way.

Ki–developing Exercise

Just like everything else, it is important to find a skilled teacher to guide you on how to do things correctly, but the following exercises will get you started until then. One method of cultivating ki is called "holding the ball." This, to me, is one of the simplest exercises to learn, but also one of the most effective. Being complex is not always better. Also remember that every person will have a slightly different experience, so if you feel something different than I describe or nothing at all, it does not necessarily mean that it is not working or you are doing something wrong. Continue to practice regularly without judgment or expectations, and just empty the mind of thought.

Observe any sensations or changes that may occur any-where in the body. Remember, all one has to do is breathe, and the rest of life will happen on its own.

To start this exercise, stand with your feet shoul-der–width apart. The back and neck should be straight, imagining that the top of the head is being pulled up to the ceiling by a chain and similarly, the tailbone is being drawn to the floor. The knees should be slightly bent. Next, place the hands in front of the body at approxi-mately waist height, with the palms facing inward and the fingers extended but relaxed.

The key in the beginning is to use your imagination to visualize what is going on. This will help unify the mind, breath, and body. First, feel the connection between the floor and the bottoms of your feet. Imagine that your tail-bone is being anchored into the earth as a way to keep you rooted and grounded. As you breathe, feel the connection between your hands. Picture that there is a ball of bright energy floating between them. Simultaneously visualize that consecutive fingers on each hand are connected with light and/or electricity. As you inhale, imagine pulling in bright, healthy energy into the palms, up the arms, and into the energy center in the lower abdomen called the *hara*. As you exhale, send the energy back up the arms and out of the fingertips. With each breath, think about making the ball in between your hands grow and become more intense. Eventually, after much practice, a meditative state will happen on its own. At that time there should be no thought, just stillness. While doing the "holding the ball" exercise, you may notice a tingling of the fingertips, a temperature change, and or a feeling of magnetism pulling or repelling your hands. All of these are normal. If you do not feel anything, that is normal as well. The goal is not to feel a sensation; the goal is to increase the ki in the body to improve overall health. Just let it happen on its own. The harder you focus on trying to feel it, the longer it may take.

Another common Aikido exercise that demonstrates ki extension is the "unbendable arm."

Unbendable arm exercise done correctly

When done incorrectly, the arm will bend

During this ki exercise, the nage stands in a *hanmi* (half–body stance) with one foot forward and the same side arm extended in front of him. The uke faces the nage and allows him to rest his wrist on his shoulder, while the uke places his hands over nage's elbow. The uke then attempts to bend the arm of the nage by pulling it downward. During the exercise, the nage should breathe and be relaxed with his arm slightly bent while focusing on a point beyond his fingertips. Imagine all of the energy from the universe flowing through your arm, supporting it, so that nothing can bend it. If the nage can extend his ki successfully, the arm will not bend. "Unbendable arm" is accomplished only when there is no muscle tension in the arm and the body is relaxed.

Sometimes people have the feeling that their minds are in a constant state of chaos. I find the following exercise to be a good method to calm the mind down. The starting position can be either standing or in *seiza* (seated position).

First begin by taking a few deep breaths in through the nose and out of the mouth while imagining filling the body with air starting from the lower abdomen and moving all the way up to the chest. Be aware of any restrictions or discomfort in the body, but do not place judgment to what you feel. Once breathing becomes fluid, with inhalation and exhalation transitioning smoothly, the actual movements can begin. As you inhale, move your arms up laterally to the top of the head as you imagine scooping in healthy white energy with the palms. The inhalation should be timed properly so the hands reach the top of the head, palms facing inward, as the inhalation finishes. At this point, visualize energy between the hands.

As exhalation begins, move the hands downward until the breath ends and the hands reach the hara. As the hands are moving down, imagine moving the healthy energy through the body, washing away any blockages or impurities that you may sense. Additionally, visualize that each pass brings the body further into stillness, like calming the ripples of a pond. Continue to do this as long as possible, until there is a sense of total relaxation and calmness. The mind should no longer feel out of control. -

In truth, there should be no mystery as to whether ki exists; rather, we should only consider the limitless possibilities that can be realized through sincere and persistent practice. Ki can help people connect with one another in a profound way that is unlike any other and provide a method of better understanding ourselves. True Aikido stems from the ki of heaven and earth ergo there is no Aikido without ki. As you practice Aikido, enjoy the exploration of ki with sincerity and honesty.

先生

What is a Sensei?

I was teaching a lesson during a children's' class at my dojo when I asked the students, "Why are you studying the martial arts?" I was quickly bombarded with answers ranging from "for fun" to "for self-defense and discipline." Then one young boy raised his hand and replied, "To keep the arts alive." I knew immediately that this child, at such a young age, had the makings of a great sensei.

The role of the martial arts instructor, otherwise known as a *sensei,* is like no other. In Japanese, *"sensei"* can be interpreted as "teacher," but a sensei is much more than that. As with any teacher, their role is to convey information in an unbiased and easily comprehendible and efficient way. A skilled sensei will do this with the martial arts he teaches, acting as a guide and pointing the way for his students along both a physical and spiritual journey. A sensei can be a mentor, a disciplinarian, a father figure, and a friend. He is all of these. During a student's lifelong pursuit, a sensei knows when to be stern and also when to show compassion without personal attachment to the outcome. He also knows how to set boundaries, preventing students from becoming too personal. That may break down the natural hierarchy that is an important aspect of martial arts training.

Through a sensei's own practice and skill, he will inspire students so there is no need to overcorrect them or make them into robot copies. In fact, if a sensei gives his student all the answers, it is the student who will suffer more than benefit. The sensei must let the student find his own way along the path. However, students by nature will try to emulate their teacher, maintaining consistency within the dojo. It is true that a sensei will often add his own flavor to the art based on his personal life experiences, but changing from the original methods of doing things causes the art to become altered into something it was not intended, no longer preserving it.

Teaching Children

When I first began teaching children, I made the mistake that many instructors make at some point. I tried to teach them as adults. I had a preconceived idea that my children were going to be super disciplined, super focused, and apparently super mini–soldiers of sorts. As my kids' class started to dwindle, I knew I was doing something wrong. My heart was in the right place because I really wanted them to learn and achieve something that had personally given me so much. However, the children were so turned off by the rigidity of my teaching that they became resistant to the information. I knew that if I did not change something soon, I would have no children left to instruct.

One of the first things I did to change was so simple, and yet very effective. I smiled. I went from the "scary sensei" to someone they could have fun with. I made it a point to enjoy teaching kids. It was not that I did not enjoy teaching them before, but I felt it difficult to keep their attention, and so it was a little disheartening. Next, I thought about ways to make the lessons fun while continuing to teach the necessary skills. In addition to the regular paired practice, I created obstacle courses to practice falling and rolling, self–defense exercises during which kids jump out and attack each other to develop reaction time and spontaneity of technique, and also fun speed drills. As I evolved, my children did also. They wanted to come to class and still learned what they needed. Surprisingly, I was still able to maintain the children's discipline and focus, but now they were not fighting me to learn. I know these are not new ideas, but for someone who likes things to be done in a very traditional and regimented manner, it was profound for me. It forced me to grow as an instructor and open my mind to another complementary mode of thought.

When teaching children, communication is key. By speaking in a calm and unthreatening manner, children often respond in kind. No child should be shown preference or ignored either. For success, a sensei should show equality for all. When children feel neglected, they often try to overcompensate. In response, they can act out because they are craving attention, whether positive or negative, or they may lose interest in classes all together. When a child becomes overconfident through favoritism, he can become a discipline problem. Therefore, humility, courtesy, and integrity must constantly be emphasized.

On occasion, there is an unruly student that needs to be disciplined. After giving a warning, I recommend having clear, predetermined consequences that are always enforced. Consistency seems to earn a student's respect and defines what is expected of him. Try to make the consequence difficult enough that it motivates the student to change the behavior, but one that also strengthens the student and does not hurt him. For instance, doing push-ups can be tiring, but it helps develop strong muscles. Striking a student with a stick may be effective and common in some dojos, but it is a bad punishment. It is also one that could result in a lawsuit.

Perception and Intuition in Teaching

While running a dojo, we as sensei need to be both perceptive and intuitive to what is going on with our students. Do not be deaf to what our students are telling us. Listen to what they are saying as well as what they are not saying. I know a sensei is not a therapist, but by learning how to detect the subtle nuances in our students, we can more easily transmit information, make them feel like they are noticed and cared about, and even correct a situation before a student decides to quit. Imagine how many more students would continue their training if someone caught the problem initially.

There have been several of my students who continue to come to class because I noticed slight changes in enthusiasm and body language. Some students only have a slight shift in their attitude when they walk in, but a perceptive sensei can often recognize these signals. When a problem is detected, a sensei must distinguish how the student will react when approached about it, so choose wisely when addressing the situation. Some students need that head–on approach in order for your words to sink in and realize that quitting is not always the best option. Other more shy students need to believe that they discovered for themselves that they want to continue.

Several years ago, I had a student I believed would quit if something was not done. He needed the head–on approach. His attendance was dwindling until I confronted him. I asked, "When you started classes, didn't you want to be able to defend yourself effectively?"

Of course he answered, "Yes."

In order for him to look inward and think about his goals, I replied with another common sense question. "How are you going to do that if you are not in class?" With a dumbfounded expression on his face, he knew that he had been making lame excuses and began to come regularly.

Another student I taught had to be handled more subtly. I saw that she enjoyed classes but felt insecure in her abilities as a martial artist and a person. Due to her insecurities, she was making excuses in her mind that she should stop training because she would never be any good. This was not true, but she needed to see for herself that she was progressing as a student. Although she never directly said this to me, it was evident that she felt this way by the way she held herself in and out of class.

One day she came in early under the auspices of having to ask me a question. However, I knew that it was her attempt to quit. Before she could reach that point, I asked her to be in a demonstration that the dojo was doing. I decided to ask her days before, but the timing was crucial because she needed to feel like she was part of something of value in order to counteract the negative emotions. After the demo, her attitude started to improve, and years later she is still a member of the dojo today.

Losing Students

Day to day, a sensei's lessons can influence his students. That is why it is important to send a positive message through his teachings. Instead of destroying a student's confidence through negative criticism, turn their weaknesses into strengths and praise them for the things they do well. Students appreciate this method and try twice as hard to please. This positive energy can resonate through the dojo and its members in a contagious way, improving the quality of training for everyone. Potential students who are looking for a school will sense this and be eager to join. Unfortunately, there are times when a student decides to leave the dojo and discontinue training. The truth is that students will quit for many reasons or for no reason at all. Whatever the case, a sensei should not take the loss of a student personally as long as his intentions are good.

Due to the bond that can naturally develop, it can be hard to let go when a student wants to quit his training.

Yes, the financial aspect is of course an upsetting factor because every time you lose a student, there is a monetary loss, but it is more than that. As a sensei, you put your heart, mind, and spirit into helping your students grow. When they leave, it is unfortunate that they will no longer benefit from what Aikido has to offer. As sensei we must learn to let go of the quitters and focus on the achievements of the focused and dedicated students. This is not to say that the quitters are unimportant as individuals, but holding on to that type of negativity can often foster feelings of anger and resentment as well as inadequacy as an instructor.

I remember looking at a plant in my room as I gave a massage to a client. As I gazed on the plant, I noticed that although the bottom leaves were starting to die off, the plant was growing healthier than ever. I realized that as in nature, we must allow the lost students to "die off" in order for the dojo to grow stronger as a whole. The result will be a dojo filled with dedicated and hard–working individuals who are willing to learn the information in a positive way.

As sensei we cannot save every student. It is out of ego to think that we can. It is the students who need to save themselves. We can only show them the door to a certain way of life, but they must choose whether or not to walk through. For some it is too hard, and they would much rather hop from one activity to the next, becoming masters of nothing. If and when they are ready, they will return to continue what they started.

Many less–experienced instructors may take it as a personal attack when a student does something in contrast with their ideals, but it is the wise teacher who deals with the situation in accordance with the philosophy of *budo* (martial ways) without resentment, embarrassment, or plans of retaliation. As a role model, he must teach through example, living his own life in accordance with the path he embodies to his students. This creates trust because the student sees that the sensei has confidence in what he teaches, and therefore so will his disciples. For a sensei to say one thing and live another way is hypocritical.

Students should realize that with martial arts training, they put their lives in their sensei's hands, so they must have complete faith in their teacher. The sensei should also recognize the amount of trust that it takes to do this and will therefore not abuse this trust. A sensei may even put his personal feelings aside, placing the needs of the individual student, the organization with which he is affiliated, and the art before his own. This is not an easy task, but a sensei wants his students to excel.

During my Brooklyn days, a father and son came into my school. They told me up front that they were studying under another sensei, but they were thinking about studying something else instead. After taking my class, they thanked me and told me how much they enjoyed it and assured me that I would hear from them soon.

About two weeks later, I got a strange knock on the door before one of my classes. When I opened the door, the older gentlemen introduced himself as the founder of some weird style of mixed martial arts and the instructor of the father and son that tried my class two weeks prior. He came up to me and said, "Do you remember those two students who tried your class without my permission? Well I gave them such a beating that they won't do that again." It is true that the students should have asked their sensei first before going to visit another dojo, but beating your students is both extreme and inappropriate.

"So, what can I do for you?" I asked.

He requested permission to watch the class, but instead I told him, "Why don't you get on the mat and participate?" No sooner did I finish my sentence than he was shaking his head "no." Instead, he stood on the side, trying to mimic my movements with his hands. Once the class was over, I asked him what he thought, and he said he liked what he had seen. I then walked him out of the dojo and asked him to say hello to his students for me. This sensei obviously felt a loss of control and had to intimidate his students in an attempt to regain it. However, there are much better ways to get respect, especially since having control over a student is only an illusion.

Earning Respect from Students

When a sensei wants to earn the respect of his pupils, there are generally two methods to accomplish this. The first way is through fear and intimidation. Some sensei will insult a student in a condescending manner or cause the student pain in order to correct their behavior while flaunting their self–conceived superiority in order to inflate their ego. Since it should be obvious that a teacher who has studied for several years could disable his students, why is there a need to bully them into submission? This does not mean a student should never be disciplined, but rather corrected using more productive means. A more effective way of accomplishing change is by giving respect back to the student and teaching them the martial way. Train and teach with sincerity, and students will respect you because of your knowledge and skill. Also, making a student look inward by questioning their actions can affect the student outwardly.

Sometimes during training, students will try to test a sensei's ability to defend themselves. They may intentionally try to strike or pin their instructor in an attempt to improve their self–confidence or to bring that illusionary concept of the untouchable teacher closer to their grasp, in order to gauge how they have progressed. The problem is that if the sensei treats this situation with the 100 percent intensity needed to subdue an aggressive attack, there is a good chance he may injure his student. On the other hand, if the sensei does not do what is needed, he either risks injury to himself or at the very least may look unskilled in front of his students. Beginner students can sometimes view this as weakness and may even want to leave the dojo because of it.

What those students do not see is that a good sensei does not need to hurt his students. Rather, it is out of gentleness and compassion for an inexperienced student that control is demonstrated. This is with the understanding that if the sensei truly defended themselves with real strikes and full power throws, the result would produce a more successful outcome. The reality is even the best sensei may get hit, thrown, or cut. We are only human, and we continue to learn and occasionally make mistakes. The idea is to not let it affect our attitudes.

Responsibility to Keep Martial Arts Alive

When looking at the bigger picture, it is the sensei who perpetuates the survival of the martial arts. This is why it is so important to teach. When teaching, there is no need to withhold techniques from students in fear of them surpassing you, because if they are withheld for too long they may eventually be lost to the next generation. Instead, pass information to those students who work diligently for it. If a student excels beyond his teacher, that sensei should be proud because it means he did his job extremely well. At the same time, a sensei should continue to train to improve his skills, which will prevent that from happening. When a student surpasses his instructor because his teacher does not continue to train regularly, it shows laziness unbecoming of one who supposedly points the way for so many others.

Up through my *nidan* (second–degree black belt), I was teaching classes at my teacher's school in Brooklyn, which was a great experience. Then one day he pulled me aside and said, "It's time for you to leave the nest. Go open your own school." At first I did not understand why, because I felt that there were so many more lessons that I could learn. When I voiced my concern to him, he replied, "You are always welcome here, but your obligation is to the arts now. If they are to be kept alive, you must help to spread them yourself."

In hindsight I realize this is the best thing he could have done for me. Soon after these words of advice, I moved from New York City to Whitehall, Pennsylvania, where I opened my current school. It is during this time that a student becomes a leader, stepping out from their teacher's shadow in order to develop their own identity as martial artists. This move also forced me to refine my technique, because without my sensei being easily accessible, the answers to my students' questions had to come from me. If I did not truly understand how to break down each technique and teach them effectively, the art would be presented poorly and therefore deteriorate. I had to attract my own set of students and also learn about the business aspect of running a martial arts school. Soon after the grand opening of my dojo several years ago, I received my *sandan* (third–degree black belt), which I attribute to this eye–opening experience.

It is inspiration, not intimidation that allows a teacher to touch others. It is time that we as sensei work together in order to uphold the high standard that martial arts were based upon. As long as our intent stays pure and free from ego, we can send a positive message to Aikido enthusiasts around the world.

認識

Awareness

People often believe that they are observant, but ask them to describe something they saw in passing only an hour ago. By simply being aware, many problems can be avoided. How many times has there been a car accident because people were talking on their cell phones instead of watching the road? People are being assaulted or pick pocketed all the time because they do not notice the warning signs. In fact, criminals choose targets because they perceive those who are unaware. Since criminals look like everyone else, it is their behavior that must be discerned through a sea of sensory information from our everyday lives. When people get too caught up in what they are doing or where they are going, it is easy to lose sight of what is right in front of them.

Part of being aware is having awareness of oneself. Understand that having awareness is not the same as acting paranoid; it is a state of calmness in which a person can evaluate a situation or another's intent objectively.

The French philosopher Descartes once said, "I think, therefore I am," but I want to go a step further and say, "I am aware of what I think, therefore I am aware of who I am." It is not enough to be conscious; we must also realize what we are thinking and act ethically and rationally upon those thoughts. By recognizing our thoughts, we can take control of them.

Awareness of our Body

When a person can notice her own posture, gait, and muscular tensions, she can take the proper steps to refine them. After musculoskeletal corrections are made, balance, reaction time, and everyday activities, including martial arts training, become easier and more efficient. These kinds of changes can be achieved through the appropriate placement of the feet, correct dispersion of weight, aligning the spine, and maintaining the body by getting regular bodywork like massage and/or acupuncture in order to improve overall structural health.

As a massage therapist, I have found that the amount of bodywork a person receives affects how in tune to their body they are. Just as a car needs an oil change every three thousand miles, the human body needs regular maintenance. The more often an individual keeps these issues in check, the more connected to their body they will be. Keep in mind that it is more difficult to be aware of our surroundings and others around us if we are not first aware of ourselves. However, this does not mean we should be so self–absorbed that we lose sight of everything else.

People who listen to their bodies are more able to detect problems and are more willing to attempt correcting them at the onset instead of letting them escalate. Additionally, people who are more aware of their bodies will, as a result, eat healthier and do things to strengthen their constitution.

Increasing Awareness

You may be wondering, "How do I become more aware?" Meditation is one method that helps to develop awareness of the mind, the body, the spirit, and the link between all three. In Aikido, an aikido–ka develops an awareness of her own and other people's body language, her surroundings, and the relation between them. It is possible through rigorous practice to achieve an acute awareness by reading cues in body language. The subtle body shifts and facial expressions that a person makes, as well as changes in breathing and/or how one telegraphs a strike, are indicators that a trained person can see. By having realistic fast–paced training, the mind will naturally develop the ability to read these signs and therefore become more prepared to effectively deal with whatever attack may come. This skill will be further refined as the mind learns to process the stimuli of various strikes and body movements more quickly, until the body can react instinctively.

Through constant Aikido practice, a person also learns how to empty the mind, maximizing the mind–body connection, so her body can avoid the attack altogether. Some long–time practitioners have even developed a perception that seems beyond the norm.

Perceiving Danger

Since victory in combat becomes far more likely when the person is able to successfully perceive the attack, recognition of a threat should happen from the moment that there is intent. By quieting the mind, one can sense when something is out of balance or when a bad situation might arise. A quiet and aware mind allows for those few extra seconds that may mean the difference between having a successful defense or not. At the highest levels of developing awareness, a skilled aikido–ka can discern a threat before physical movement is initiated by perceiving the extension of ki (internal energy).

Again, the extension of ki has to do with a palpable projection of energy that the body radiates. This occurs at the time of intent, right before an attack is initiated. The attack, and therefore the extension of ki, occurs once there is intent since the mind controls the body. However, before a person can attain this kind of sensitivity, she must take attention away from her own internal chatter and focus on connecting with all that surrounds her.

When I began training in New York City, my teacher held class in a run–down community center located in a subsection of New York called Alphabet City. For those who do not know about that section of town, it is not the safest neighborhood at night. One day I was teaching class because my teacher was at a seminar. As I began leading the warm–ups, I heard a weird cracking sound and quickly decided to move from where I stood. As I turned, something flew about an inch from my face. When I peered behind me, I saw a man from a local gang lying on a nearby rooftop with a pellet rifle in his hand. He shot again. The pellet broke through the glass window and I luckily dodged that one as well. "Get down!" I yelled, telling everyone to move away from the window. Next I shouted at the so–called sniper, and eventually he took off running. If I had been so wrapped up in class that I did not perceive what was going on around me and hadn't shifted out of the way, I could have been injured badly.

From the minute you enter a new environment, take notice of what is going on. Since a person is flooded with information, they must filter out the sensory noise from the important facts. If you are in an unfamiliar place, it is necessary to eliminate distractions and focus on what is going on around you. When a person acts like a tourist, they give off signals to predators that make them potential targets. Instead, make an assessment of where any exits are, and if there are any other possible dangers. Look around to see if there are people that stand out as being aggressive or make you feel uncomfortable. If so, leave. By removing yourself, you remove the potential danger. Although some may see it as a sign of weakness to leave, I believe it to be a sign of intelligence. It is only when circumstances beyond our control arise with no way out that it is time to fight. Nevertheless, if one does not notice the problem early enough to leave then they were probably not observant enough.

Applying Awareness in All Areas

In the dojo, one must use her awareness and apply them to all things. For example, if a person is unaware while performing an act of etiquette, there is the possibility of showing disrespect toward another classmate or instructor if done incorrectly. Moreover, the students who are not observant may miss vital parts of a technique being demonstrated, making the student's execution ineffective. They could also miss blocking a strike that could be potentially dangerous. More advanced students are able to perceive the subtleties of a technique after only one or two demonstrations, whereas students who are less experienced take several times to review even the most basic techniques. Skillful observers do not allow their minds to wander and use their cognitive abilities to assess the important stimuli around them. Awareness in the dojo comes from perceiving things initially, not by being corrected after it is too late.

Part of being aware is using all of our senses, including our intuition. There is a palpable feeling when negativity is in a room, so we can use it to help ensure our safety. I remember walking into a room as a child after two people were arguing and feeling the uneasiness in the air, even though I never actually heard them speak. We all have had a "gut feeling" that could not be explained rationally, but by trusting it we benefited. Whether it was a possible investment that paid off, a bad feeling about a person that you met, or taking a different path than usual when walking home after work, there may be a subconscious signal that was picked up on.

Then why do people not trust their intuition? I assume that part of the reason is that there is little to no research with proven empirical data on intuition, at least none that I have seen. On occasion, some of our "gut feelings" may be unfounded, but this does not mean that we cannot benefit from listening to intuition or learn to incorporate it into our daily lives. We were given this ability as part of our natural instinct to survive, so we need to cultivate this important gift. Unfortunately in our society, people are encouraged to ignore this part of our awareness instead of embracing it, in the name of science. The movie *Contact* presented a similar question: "Could you prove to a scientist that you loved someone empirically?" Most probably could not, but love does exist. Just because something cannot be proven does not mean it is not there. Intuition, one aspect of awareness, is a vital tool in a human's arsenal of perception skills if the time is taken to listen to it.

There were several times where listening to my intuition has worked for me, but one stands out in particular. When I lived in Manhattan, my cousin and I played billiards in SoHo after class. Every week, almost religiously, we went on the same day and played. However, one evening, we both decided for no particular reason that this week we were just going to go home. The next morning my cousin called me sounding quite excited, "Did you hear what happened at the billiards place?" I had not. He told me that two guys walked in and started shooting people at the billiard hall. Several people were injured, and a few were even killed. Now, some may call it luck, but the fact that on that specific night, after months of going regularly, we decided to change our routine seems more than a coincidence to me. We never returned to that hall again.

Being aware means we should observe ourselves, others, our surroundings and the relationship between them in an intelligent and unbiased way. Awareness is the first step toward eliminating potentially harmful situations and diffusing them when they do arise. In scenarios where self–defense is needed, awareness includes the perception of an attack before it has fully manifested. All in all, being a good aikido–ka is being successful in the art of awareness.

受容

Acceptance

My grandmother always used the cliché, "If you have lemons, make lemonade," because there are things in life that happen to us, some good and some bad. It is how we deal with these moments that helps determine our success in life. It is useless to try to control what will happen to us because control is an illusion. We can no sooner control our surroundings than we could the wind. If we truly had control, why would we choose to be sick, lose a loved one, or get mugged?

"What is the point of trying then?" you may ask. The point is not to try to control everything, but rather to make good decisions harmoniously with our true nature and then accept the outcome. We are often given situations in life that we may consider tragic, but I have often found that they are merely the lessons that we need to learn in order to move forward. Sometimes the universe seems to provide these lessons in succession with increasing intensity with one right after the next. This may be the universe's way of beating people over the head with those lessons until they make the necessary changes. People frequently resist change, but all things must change or die. This is how we grow and evolve. Accept that change will happen, but make the choice to change for the better.

Fire vs. Fire and Water vs. Fire

In Aikido, there are many different levels of acceptance to consider, including the physical, emotional, and the spiritual. From a physical perspective, when a person trains he accepts a certain level of conditioning beyond the normal workout, because it ultimately makes him stronger. For example, some arts teach students to accept strikes to the body or various hip throws and joint locks, and although it may be uncomfortable to students in the short term, this type of training can strengthen tendons as well as toughen the body.

Also, the principles of aiki, or unifying with the ki of an attacker, are applied strategies that use the concept of acceptance in combat. When someone is pushed by an attacker, he may be knocked back if he stays in the way of the push while trying to resist it. This is a fire–versus–fire mentality, as in two opposing forces going head on. This method only further escalates the situation until there is a wrestling match. As someone defending themselves, would you really want to merely stand there and take the blow? Probably not.

However, if we do not resist the attack, but instead accept and yield to it, then we are able to deal with it more effectively. This is a water–versus–fire mentality. It can be done simply by moving out of the way, parrying, or redirecting the force of the person. By accepting the attack, there is no resistance. As a result, *kuzushi* (off–balance) is created in the assailant allowing for a more efficient defense. Similarly, if we are pulled we should not resist either. By entering when we are pulled, we can use the force of the pull to perform an entering throw, forcing the attacker to use his own energy against himself. It is by applying the principles of acceptance to self–defense that a larger and stronger opponent can be subdued.

As stated earlier, this philosophy can be adapted to other aspects of our lives such as our emotional well being. We often feel the push and pull of the every day but if we deal with our emotions in a healthy manner, we are more likely to have a sense of inner peace and clarity.

For example, when an argument ensues between co–workers, there are generally two outcomes. The fire–versus–fire approach is a screaming match with each person screaming louder and louder until there is a full–out explosion. This method is pointless with usually no resolution, only fuel to the fire. Acceptance is easier. It only requires listening without judgment. If you were accused of something, do not get defensive. First, be honest with yourself and see if it is true. If so, take responsibility for your actions and improve the situation to the best of your ability. If it is not true, then do not worry about it. Either prove it to be false through fact not volume, or let it go. Holding on to that kind of negativity only increases stress and makes the situation worse while interfering with the normal happy work environment that everyone is entitled to. In either case, the situation may have actually been the initiator's issue, not yours, so do not take it personally. Consider that a stressful workplace is usually one with drama instead of understanding, so do not feed into the drama. Besides, you are there to work, not socialize.

Accepting Emotion and Outcome

It can also be difficult to accept that we cannot do everything, especially when we have to say no to another person that we care about. Feelings of guilt can arise when we have to say no, particularly because humans seem to, on some level, have an inherent need to please. Nevertheless, to try and please everyone all the time while attempting to do what you need for yourself causes stress. We feel emotionally drained, and it leaves no time for personal pursuits. People need to make time for themselves, and as long as saying no is not just an excuse for being lazy, they should not feel guilty if they cannot always handle every request. By being honest about our feelings, we spend less energy trying to hide the truth. Everyone feels emotions; it is part of the human condition. To deny them is simply denying part of our self. On the other hand, it is how we cope with our emotions that will determine our emotional stability. When a person holds on to an emotion, whether positive or negative, they become emotionally stuck, dwelling in the past. A healthier way is to make a conscious realization that the emotion exists, acknowledge it, and then return to the present so you can more readily enjoy your life in the moment. Each time an emotion comes to the surface, take notice as to what the emotion is because once a person can identify it, they can more readily discover the source of the emotion and let it go. By discovering the source, that person has the power to change it instead of allowing it to control them.

If we must fight, then we must do so with an acceptance of the outcome. If we accept that we may lose, our minds become free which allows us to defend ourselves without the preoccupation of defeat. I am not saying that a person should give up or have a defeatist attitude; however, we must understand that there is always the chance of defeat and by denying this, we are merely being naïve. One reason why the samurai were so effective in battle was because they would accept death without fear. Thus, a person with no fear is a dangerous foe. I have seen people who thought they were invincible until they were hit. Once this occurred, they became shocked and froze, which caused them to lose the fight. Even the best fighters get hit and/or cut every once in a while. The ones who are the most successful are able to accept the strike and quickly resume defending themselves until their opponent is defeated.

I once saw a video of a man who thought he was an invincible ki master because he believed that he could throw people across the room with his ki. He even offered money to anyone who could beat him, but this was a bad idea. A karate–ka took him up on his offer and gave him the surprise of his life. After the fight began, the ki master tried to throw the karate–ka with his ki by waving his hand in the air. Big surprise, it did not work. Then the karate–ka slammed him straight in the face, and the so called "ki master" just froze looking at the blood covering his face. Again, after regaining his composure, he waved his hands trying to throw his opponent. Finally the karate–ka struck him, finishing the fight with the other man crying on the floor. If the "ki master" had accepted that he might be hit and that he may be unable to throw him with ki, he could have tried something else instead of freaking out.

Emotionally, we must also accept the feelings that may arise during a confrontational situation. Some may feel anger while others may feel fear. Some may even feel joy at the thought of hurting another, but all of these emotions are usually reflections of our own internal state of being. For instance, fear of confrontation may be a manifestation of our own insecurities. To get past them, start by acknowledging why these emotions are coming to the surface, but do not let them rule you. By first accepting that they are present, you can better deal with and eliminate them.

From a spiritual perspective, it is not virtuous to judge or criticize others for their choices. Even when you have the best intentions, it is their decision and not yours. If a person is truly happy with their choice, whether another agrees or not, then it was the right choice for them. As long as the result is not hurting others or themselves, we need to show acceptance. If everyone took the time they spend on judging others and used it to work on themselves instead, the world would be a much happier and more productive place. In life there is more than one right answer so take the opportunity to learn as many answers as you can. By closing your mind to several points of view, you may also be closing the door on a wealth of useful information.

Acceptance Leads to Harmony

In the dojo, we must have acceptance for everyone. As aikido–ka we must trust that those we work with are not there to hurt us, but instead to help us learn. It is important to accept those who are too rough, those who are very timid, the unskilled and the exceptional all the same. Even if we do not like them as people, we should accept them because they have the same goal as you—to learn.

A similar case occurred in my dojo many years ago, which needed to be remedied between two children who

I will call Scott and Paul. Paul had attended the dojo for several years. In the beginning, Paul was quite rough, whined constantly, and tried whatever he could to do the minimum amount of exercise in class to get by. Nobody wanted to work with Paul. In fact, other children quit because they could not tolerate being around him. I knew Paul was a good kid who merely needed some focus as well as a little compassion. As time progressed, so did Paul. His technique improved and he complained less during class. Things were getting better.

Eventually, another boy named Scott joined the dojo. Scott was twelve years old and suffered from severe attention deficit disorder (ADD). His parents signed him up in the hopes that the martial arts would help him to get his disorder under control. Scott was awkward in his body movements and his mind was all over the place, but I could see that he wanted to improve. I decided that Paul and Scott should try to work together in the hopes that Paul would be sympathetic to Scott's situation and perhaps become a positive role model for him. Unfortunately, that did not work well at all. Scott, because of his inexperience, accidentally hit Paul and threw him down quite hard. Luckily, Paul was not injured. Although Scott apologized several times, Paul would not forgive him.

Weeks later after talking to the both of them, I put them together again to see if they could work it out, but again Paul complained. I spoke to Scott and his parents about learning control, and Scott assured me that he liked

Paul and would try to improve. Soon after, Paul came to me and said he was thinking about quitting the dojo because the class was not fun if Scott was there. When I heard this, I knew Paul needed to learn about acceptance. I told Paul that I was disappointed in his attitude and that Scott was not intentionally hurting him. I also reminded him of what he was like when he was a beginner. "Well I quit my last dojo because I didn't like a boy," he said to me smugly.

My response to this was, "By running away every time things get hard, you spend your whole life running. You may decide to leave here, but no matter where you go, there is eventually going to be someone that you do not like so it is better that we handle it now. Stop threatening to quit every time things do not go your way and let's make a friend out of someone who needs one because don't you have enough enemies?" He then asked if he could be excused to the bathroom. When he was done, he came out and continued to participate with the rest of the class.

Surprisingly, during the next exercise, Paul started to cheer Scott on with words of encouragement. I was glad to see that Paul internalized what I had said; I hope it is something that he will always remember.

Acceptance is an exploration of self because in order to have it, we must be comfortable with ourselves first. It is a common defense mechanism to resist the ideas, opinions, and/or the physical attacks from others, but it is not the way of budo. A true warrior has an open mind and an open heart and can therefore live in harmony with others and their environment. He also travels along the road of least resistance and as a result, has little or no inner turmoil. Acceptance is a path toward friendship and we all have too many enemies. Now is the time to begin.

自我

Avoiding Ego

The dojo must be an environment free of ego in order for a school to run successfully. One bad student can spoil the atmosphere of the dojo, just like a bad apple in a basket, and if taken to extremes, may even sour the enthusiasm of the teacher. Conversely, a bad sensei can leave the students feeling empty or disheartened with their training. He may ultimately turn them off to the martial arts all together. Ego can be the thing that ruins the individual and the bunch.

When discussing ego, one must also address the concept of confidence. Confidence is having trust in something or someone, whereas ego is an over–exaggerated sense of self–importance. An aikido–ka with confidence knows that his techniques work and allows his skills to speak for him. He needs to prove nothing. An aikido–ka with an ego speaks in order to convince others of how good he is. This benefits no one. It is good to have confidence, not ego.

Often prospective students come into my school to try a free class, and unfortunately they sometimes have an ego. When I taught in Brooklyn, New York, one of these people came in. He eagerly told me how he had been studying Jeet Kune Do (Bruce Lee's martial art) for some time; however, when I asked him who his previous teacher was, he said he was self–taught from a book. Now, any martial artist knows it is ridiculous to try to learn martial arts in that way, because a real teacher is needed as a guide for learning proper technique, making corrections, and explaining how to make the art work effectively. Anyway, I gave him the benefit of the doubt, assuming that he had a sincere interest to learn, and I allowed him to try my class. When the lesson ended, my teacher, who happened to be watching, asked him if he liked the class. "Oh yes, I like it, but I think I could master the whole system in about three months," he responded. I could not believe that he had the disrespect to tell us that or the ego to believe it.

After our jaws dropped at the shock of the response, my teacher just grinned. He reached into his desk and placed $100 on his desk. He then said, "Not only do I know that you could not master the art in three months, but I don't think you can even block one punch. If you can block one of David, Sensei's punches, I will give you this $100 dollars. He will even tell you with which hand he is going to hit you, when he is going to hit you, and where."

The man, with a smug look on his face, agreed. While smiling from the pure peculiarity of the whole situation, I told him I would hit him with my left hand in the chest. "Are you ready?" I asked.

"Yep," he replied. In an instant, I snapped out my punch and hit him square in the chest. "Wait, I wasn't ready!"

So I asked him again, "Are you ready now? Because I will do the exact same thing." He shook his head, and once again he got one in the exact same spot.

He then said, "Well, I could have elbowed you in the head." I told him that if he wanted one more chance, I would be happy to let him try to elbow me in the head while blocking my punch. Of course, he failed.

Afterward, we told him that if he was willing to put his ego aside and learn sincerely, he was welcome to come back. We never heard from him again.

Rank and Ego

In the dojo, a member's rank can be a major source of ego. Conflicts arise when students feel entitled to more rank and/or power than they have earned, but there is a chain of command in Aikido just like in the military including generals, privates, and even a president. This methodology is not only important because it is part of the martial arts experience, but also because of its efficacy at maintaining structure and humility. When there is no respect for the dojo structure, it will eventually break down and chaos will start to ensue.

In the dojo hierarchy there is one headmaster. He is usually, but not always, a shihan. The headmaster is like a general reporting to his superior and teacher, commonly a soke. Otherwise he is in charge of the decisions for the dojo. Under the shihan are the sensei. The sensei are those teachers who report to the shihan. The sensei are in charge of assisting the shihan and may be involved in various tasks like teaching classes to low–ranking students or administrative work that is needed to be finished. Lastly, there are the students. There are upper–, middle–, and lower–level students, who, at the beginning and end of each class, line up according to that rank. The mudansha (student ranks) are responsible for attending class to continue their education. Additionally, they are expected to clean the dojo and help with whatever else is needed. No matter what rank a person has, he must be humble. Keep in mind that it is considered disrespectful to question the teachings or choices of those higher in rank, as long as they are ethical and legal.

I want to share another story about a student I had about five years ago. He had moved through the ranks fairly quickly and had become one of the more advanced students in the dojo. He had earned certain privileges that students of his rank attain, and so he most likely considered himself "a big fish" in our "little pond." As such, I invited him and other senior students on a trip to Japan in order to train with my teacher and other renowned instructors in the organization. This person was the only one who decided to go. When we got to Japan, it was a big wake–up call for him because he soon was exposed to the reality of traditional martial arts and the chain of command. Since he was only a student kyu rank, he was made to carry weapons to training sessions, was not invited to participate in demos, and was not allowed to attend certain meetings that my teacher and I were invited to. This is not to say he would never get those opportunities, but he just had to put in his dues first. He then realized that he was "a small fish in a much bigger pond." This can be a big blow to the ego. I felt bad that his feelings were hurt, but it was an important lesson in humility that he needed to learn. Soon after we returned, he quit coming to the dojo. Once again, ego gets in the way of knowledge.

In some cases, a student may be greedy for power and try to gain favor from those above them, but there is no place for this kind of behavior in a dojo. He may even try to circumvent the teacher and try befriending an upper–level shihan or even the soke. By attempting this, the student dishonors himself and disrespects his teacher, the upper–level instructor, and the code of conduct of the martial arts. Besides, this is usually futile. In fact, the student could easily be expelled from the dojo because he obviously is more interested in titles and rank than in sincerely learning.

Something along these lines happened to me when I first started out as a sensei. I was teaching at the same school with my teacher, who was a shihan back then. During that time, I taught different classes than my instructor and was given my own student base to be in charge of and cultivate. One of those was a brown belt student who had been with me for several years. He was not an instructor yet, although he would often help me demonstrate techniques or help the beginners if I was assisting someone else at the time. This student saw how the shihan and I had developed a close relationship due to the years of dedicated service I gave to him. Because of our relationship and my skill level, my teacher would often give me more advanced instruction and allow me to attend clinics and meetings that were off limits to lower–level students.

Then one day my shihan came to me looking upset. When I asked him what was wrong, he told me about my student. My student had gone to him behind my back and told him that he would like to have the same relation-ship with him that I had. I was shocked. Not because he hurt my pride, because I would have gladly passed on the student to the shihan if he had requested it, but because he had not learned the respect that I had tried to instill in him over the years. Luckily, my teacher made it very clear that he had not yet earned that privilege and needed to learn humility. That student left soon after the incident, which I believe was due to his ego getting in the way.

There have been instances when a person had shown up at my dojo claiming to be an expert of a certain martial art or having rank from a particular teacher. These people often ask if they can wear their rank in my dojo. Unless they are from my affiliate organizations or I know the quality of their previous instruction, I usually decline. Since they have not studied the techniques that I teach and have not demonstrated that they can perform them with the proficiency that I require, they are asked to wear a white belt. Those with big egos are often insulted at the thought of having to wear a white belt and leave; those who are humble are content to wear one because they are more interested in learning than in what is around their waist. I do not have them wear this beginner rank as a lack of respect for their achievements or because I want to keep them from earning rank; it makes no difference to me. I would be happy to do the same if our positions were reversed. Rather, I do this to maintain consistency and a higher standard. In fact, I personally enjoy the opportunity to put on a white belt because I get to train with a clean slate, free from other people's expectations. Anytime I have entered a dojo outside of my respective organizations, it was with a white belt unless asked to do otherwise.

Although it is natural to be proud when earning the next belt, make it a point to receive rank with modesty. There are always more doors that we can open, and always someone who is better than we are, so it is important to not let the ego get the better of us.

Ego Prevents Progress

When a person has an ego, it prevents him from learning all that he can. If a person believes that he always knows best, he is less likely to open his heart and mind. Everybody can learn something. No matter how experienced a person is, there is an infinite sea of knowledge available to him when he is ready to receive it. Some of the most profound lessons I have learned have been from beginners. They can react differently than a trained practitioner and often have interesting points of view. Unfortunately, too many teachers scoff at their students' comments without ever really listening to them. As long as the comment or question is presented appropriately, there is no harm in listening, and there might just be something worth hearing.

In some instances, there can be a competitive feeling between students. Although competition can motivate a person to excel, when it is taken to extremes it often leads to bitterness in some and an inflated ego in others. For example, if one student is having problems executing a technique on another student, a problem could ensue. Instead of asking the teacher for help and resolving the issue, he grows more and more frustrated until the student gives up, tries to force the technique and possibly cause an injury, or takes it as a personal attack. Just because a student does not allow a less–than–perfect technique to work does not mean he is the enemy. It does mean that more work needs to be done to perfect the technique. Accept it as a learning experience and an opportunity to refine your techniques.

When there are multiple sensei in a class, ego may get the better of one of them. Generally, when there is more than one black–belt instructor, the senior instructor is always in charge unless otherwise stated by the headmaster. However, there are times when a lower–level instructor feels the need to "flex his muscles." Inevitably, he takes it upon himself to inadvertently take control of the kyu ranks by showing how a technique should "really" be done. When a student or instructor feels the need to show his self–conceived prowess by changing the technique that was demonstrated by the senior instructor, it creates confusion and disharmony. By doing their own version of the technique, they have disrespected the senior instructor and apparently believe that they are too good to learn from the senior teacher. "Why be a part of a class if you are not willing to actually learn something?"

This kind of ego not only is a detriment to the low–level black belt, but often spoils it for the students who have to work with them. If there is information to share, bring it up appropriately to the senior instructor first, and it may be received graciously. Ultimately, it is the senior instructor who has the most experience. Even if you think you are right, listen to him with sincerity. He probably knows what needs to be done and has everyone's best interest at heart.

Competition and Ego

As students continue to train together, Aikido teaches that two aikido–ka are partners helping each other to learn instead of two opponents attacking each other. This philosophy creates a blending of energy that unifies the practitioner with the attacker. By having this mentality, there is an attitude of caring and helping each other to grow instead of competing with classmates with only ourselves in mind. I understand that in order to apply martial arts technique to a real–world situation effectively we must be exposed to resistance during training. Aikido–ka must challenge their partners and put them in life–like scenarios so they become comfortable when a confrontation happens on the street. Nevertheless, there is a time and place to practice in this way. After one of these more challenging sessions is finished, one should not have to brag or feel bitter. At the end of the day, they are both students of Aikido and will hopefully continue to be friendly.

There is enough competition in the world, so why not view the dojo as a place to evolve instead of a place to bring others down? This is indicative of how the theory of "water versus fire mentality," and "fire versus fire mentality" relate to ego. As mentioned in the chapter about acceptance, the "fire versus fire mentality" is one of competition where one fire feeds the other until an explosion occurs. This is often the case when the two people arguing both have an ego. On the other hand, in a "water versus fire mentality," the water puts out the fire, extinguishing a volatile situation. A person free from ego will either prove his point in a calm and factual manner or decide not to engage the other person at all. That way the argument is diffused. If you are not sure about how ego is representative of a "fire–versus–fire mentality," think about a sporting event when two opposing teammates start yelling about a ref's call. This can escalate into a brawl between the two people and then elevates further until the rest of the team gets involved. That could be avoided by letting go of ego.

I remember being at an international aiki seminar that included several hundred practitioners from around the world and guest instructors who taught different aspects of aiki. They came from a wide variety of lineages and backgrounds in their training and came to share their knowledge to bring aikido–ka together. In fact, it was probably one of the largest forums that I had seen where different organizations congregated in the same place. This does not normally happen due to ego getting in the way.

While participating in one of the seminars, I began training with a student from one of these different schools. As I began to practice the technique that was demonstrated by the guest instructor, the other student decided it would be more fun to try and grapple with me on the floor. My first thought, out of instinct, was to strike him, but I did not want to make waves in such a large forum. Instead, I escaped from his hold and got to my feet. He then attempted to do it again. This time I simply evaded and decided it was time to work with someone more interested in learning and less interested in proving who was a better grappler.

Sometimes people have egos out of insecurity. This sounds like an oxymoron, but there is some truth to this. Sometimes people feel the need to start fights for this very reason. The insecure egoist has to flaunt his superiority in an attempt to prove themselves to others and convince themselves of their own self–worth. All this shows is how little they really know. Usually the people that talk the most know the least.

When someone has exceptional skill, others will take notice without having to tell anyone. A good student does not bother with such trivialities because that is just time wasted that is better spent on training. Also, real masters will often sit quietly in the background watching patiently, confident in their ability without having to prove their greatness.

There are some instances where the ego comes from others who may know that a person is studying a martial art and tries to belittle them. These people attack with comments like, "Your techniques would not work in a fight," or "You would not be able to defend yourself against a certain person or weapon." If a student does not have enough confidence, this kind of passive aggression can do more harm than a physical assault. It may create self–doubt and insecurities that can permeate into other aspects of life. As long as the student trains hard with sincerity, he should have faith in himself and the martial arts methods he was taught. Besides, when it comes down to it, most verbal attackers are afraid to do anything when asked if they want to test their theories.

In a fighting scenario, one must let go of the need for victory to be successful in combat. When a person focuses on defeating another, the mind becomes distracted. The preoccupation with hurting someone else causes imbalances in the mind, the body, and the harmony of the spirit. This creates an opportunity for the opponent to seize the moment and exploit any openings that surface. An aikido–ka with an empty mind simply waits for an attack and deals with it, without fixating on winning or losing.

In Aikido and in life there is no place for ego. There are many forms of ego out there, whether it is out of an over–exaggerated sense of self–importance or from one's own insecurities. No matter what the reason, when ego is in your midst, stop it in its tracks and take the next step toward mastering your mind.

責任

Taking Responsibility

Every action has an equal and opposite reaction. This is a basic law of the universe. There is a continuous inter-action between people that occurs naturally through our relationships, our jobs, and through commerce. Whether our actions are friendly or cruel, generous or greedy, help-ful or self–involved, we affect others and in return affect ourselves. Why is it, then, that many of us do not take responsibility for our actions? It was the way of the samu-rai, and it is the way it should be now.

As martial artists, we should take accountability for our own training. "How much time do you spend prac-ticing?" It is common to see students slack off after the initial excitement of beginning their training has passed, but it is essential that they do not let it spin out of control. All of us began training for a reason, and whether or not those reasons have changed, do not allow them to slip away. It may be good enough for some people to show up to class semi–regularly, but excellence comes from continued practice both inside and out of the dojo. Consistent practice starts the path to becoming a master. However, if visiting with friends or watching television is more important than Aikido classes, then that is your choice, and not an excuse. Unfortunately, focusing on excuses instead of achievements can make our goals disappear.

Tyler was an eleven–year–old student of mine who impressed me more than many of the students who passed through my doors. He had been with me for about three years, until one day he called me at the dojo. He said, "Sensei, I appreciate all that you have taught me, but I want to pursue the guitar. I feel that I know how to defend myself thanks to you, and so I got what I needed from your teachings. Thank you for everything." Tyler had enough courage to call me without making any excuses or having his parents call for him, and he simply told me the truth. Although I am sad that I lost him as a student, I am proud that an eleven–year–old boy had learned more about taking responsibility than some adults. I met up with him five years later, and he is still studying the guitar.

Another part of Aikido training is taking ownership of our behavior. We must live with integrity in accordance with budo's moral and ethical mores. Treat others with courtesy and respect and they will return it in kind. If you hurt another classmate, apologize and if a person does something well, compliment them. The way we treat people in the dojo should also reflect how we treat others outside of the dojo. By propagating an attitude of mutual respect and openness in all aspects of life, we are doing our part to improve ourselves and the world. By respecting other cultural traditions like the martial arts, we take the first step toward peace.

There are those who would ignore the honorable ideals of budo by using the martial arts to dominate or intimidate others. Defeating someone in this way is cowardice and nothing to be proud of. A person like this is spreading negativity and has not taken responsibility for her actions. Ask yourself, "What are the implications if the victim is sent to the hospital just to make you feel better about yourself?" An aikido–ka fights when she has to in order to protect herself or a loved one. There should be no anger, fear, guilt, or joy in fighting—only a calmness of mind similar to when she is practicing at the dojo. Again, the desire to create conflict is neither moral nor beneficial. There is no point to look for a fight whether physical or not, because there is no profit in hurting others. Eventually, there is always someone stronger and more skilled than we are, and if we continue along this path, they will ultimately find us. This course of action is only to inflate the ego, and it is unnecessary for one who strives to be enlightened.

Responsibility to Preserve the Arts

As aikido–ka we must also take responsibility for preserving an art that has improved our lives. Simply training may not be not enough. When the time is right, it is necessary that students become sensei and teach. Since Aikido has only been kept alive by passing it to the next generation, we must continue to do so. Also, it is not sufficient to train for oneself; this is selfish. Instead, passing along this wealth of knowledge is the most altruistic way to give back to Aikido. Transmitting the art of Aikido in a positive way is the responsibility of the sensei and receiving the information in a positive way is the student's responsibility.

Taking Responsibility for Our Lives

When Aikido is allowed to permeate into all aspects of our lives, we can start to take ownership of it. Although, taking responsibility for our own actions is not an easy task. It is especially difficult because our ego often gets in the way. There is a tendency to rationalize a situation by putting the blame on external sources outside of our control, because then we do not have to address our own issues. Instead of acknowledging their own errors, individuals begin to pity themselves, accept complacency, and believe the illusion that they are a victim. Too often phrases like, "I'm too fat," "I do not have the will power," "I hate my job," and "I do not have enough time," are used as common excuses. Unfortunately, these are self–perpetuating lies the mind creates in order to reinforce the idea of helplessness. There are no victims.

The first step is taking responsibility for our own lives. This does not mean blame, because blame often leads to pity and depression. As adults, we have the power to decide how we live and what changes can be made to improve ourselves. We must train both our minds and bodies, striving toward a state of complete homeostasis and inner peace. The question is, "Do I want to work toward change?" As you are reading this, be aware of your own thoughts. Are phrases like, "He does not understand me and my problems," or "Easy for him to say," coming to the surface? These are excuses the mind creates as a way of deflecting issues onto others and reinforcing the negativity within ourselves. Change that attitude one thought at a time then one day at a time until you no longer fall into that abyss. Things can improve once negativity is eliminated from your life.

Emotional Crutches

When I worked in a pain management office, I often worked with people who defined themselves by their pain instead of their true selves. All they talked about to their friends and family was their pain, and by returning to the doctor's office regularly, they got someone to pay attention to them. This only further reinforced the need to experience more pain. In fact, negative emotions can hinder a physical therapeutic change while feeding the subconscious desire for more pain.

When negative emotions feed into a desire to have pain while perpetuating this vicious cycle, I call that an "emotional crutch." Interestingly, however unfortunate, many of these "pain patients" also had traumatic home life situations and/or abusive relationships without the presence of another caring individual to give them support. Nevertheless, that is not an excuse that validates this kind of behavior. In fact, many patients that I worked on had their pain return only after realizing that there was as much as a 70 to 80 percent improvement in their overall pain level. It was like a light switch turning off because in the beginning there were noticeable positive physical and energetic changes that were occurring—not to mention they were thrilled with how good they felt when they left. Suddenly, when it was time to discharge them or they saw that they were not getting the same attention from their families they would "shut off" and convince themselves that the therapy was not working. Since the mind to a large extent controls the body, I believe that their subconscious did not want to get better. I know this sounds strange because who would not want to get better, but recovering would mean letting go of what had previously defined them and force them to deal with their deeper psychological issues. Disconnecting from the deeper issues is not only unconstructive and hurtful to the individual, but their negative emotions can spread infectiously to those around them.

Have you ever been around someone who is just depressing and energetically draining to be near? Some people find it easier to deal with the physical pain than the emotional kind because they can blame their emotional state on a physical ailment, an injury, a disease, or aging instead of taking responsibility for their internal state of being. I am not saying that all chronic pain patients are like this, but I have that found many of them are.

These emotional crutches, if not dealt with, can eventually manifest as a more severe disease within the body. There are, however, those individuals who are sincere and willing to do the work needed to improve. Remember, we are not just a bunch of uncontrolled responses. We have the choice to drop negativity as one would drop a bag of bricks. By looking inward at our own issues and taking responsibility for our own thoughts and actions, we can start the healing process.

Change

The key to change is discipline and self–motivation. This is a difficult task, but it is not unattainable for those willing to work. Part of changing is having the willpower to put forth a sincere effort and stop lying to oneself. It is an uphill battle because any profound lifestyle change tests the mental resolve of the individual. For example, when a person is complaining about her weight, she needs to ask herself what changes are being made to lose that weight.

Is there a change in diet, or do you just need that dessert or larger portion? Is there regular weekly exercise, or is it just "too hard"? The choices *we* make decide the outcome. It is true that there are genetic traits and medical exceptions that predispose people toward certain physical characteristics, but there are still things that can be done to improve the overall quality of life. The real choice in this instance is health or excuses. Those who want health will seek it out, those who are not willing to do the work will not. If a person chooses disease, he or she should accept that choice instead of complaining or blaming others for their failure, because ultimately they were the ones who made that decision.

Next, take responsibility to achieve your goals. The world is full of endless possibilities for those who have the initiative to take them. A person who takes a balanced approach to life can have a career and a family and still do the things that she enjoys. When a person complains that she does not have enough time, it is because she does not make the time. It is a process of trade–offs. One must decide what activities are the most important and find how to make them fit through time management. By dedicating time to achieve more lofty goals in one aspect of her life, there must be a realistic expectation to sacrifice elsewhere. There is a conscious decision to work or play and a need to balance both. If the excuse is that your job keeps you from doing what you want, then accept that it is your choice to work there. There are other companies with salaries and benefits that are hiring; one just has to be patient and look hard enough. It may mean you have to travel or relocate to do it, but again, that may be the necessary trade–off to be able to do the other activities that you enjoy.

Also take responsibility for how you interact with others. Like ripples in a pond, one person affects the next. Just think about when someone is cut off while driving. I have seen situations in which, after an incident, the person involved becomes angered and her mood changes for the rest of the day. Next, the angered person is cold and nasty toward a waiter at lunch who in turn yells at his girlfriend for no real reason when he gets home. One person affects the next, and we do make a difference individually, whether it is for better or for worse.

Therefore, we must stop making excuses and take accountability for how we treat others as well as ourselves. If you are holding resentment toward people that you are in contact with or things in your life that you are doing, that negative energy not only affects your own emotional state, but others with whom you interact. It does not matter if you are justified in feeling this way—that is irrelevant. The truth is that you probably do not like experiencing these feelings anyway and they are not good for you. If you do not do something to change your internal conflict, whether it is by speaking to the person who is causing the stress or changing the things that you are resenting, then you are not taking responsibility and therefore need to let the negativity go.

Honoring Your Word

According to the philosophy of Aikido, it is also important to honor our word. Far too often, people of today make promises or guarantees that they will do something, only to postpone or renege altogether when the time comes to follow through. More and more people give assurances as a means to make a sale or to get another person off their back with no real concern for the outcome.

How many times have you hired a contractor or business to do a job only to find it was not finished on time or the result was not of the quality you expected? Has a friend or family member promised to do something only to be too busy when he/she were really needed? By not honoring our word, the trust between people begins to break down and the "every man for himself" attitude becomes a more prevalent problem. It is better to be honest about our inability to do something rather than to destroy our credibility. It is time to rebuild our integrity as a society and take pride in our actions, our jobs, and ourselves.

Recently, I hired Fry's fencing company to install a fence around my backyard. Fry's bid was one of the least expensive I had found, so I decided to give him a chance. The day before it was time for him to start the work, his wife called and said he was in the hospital with kidney stones. They were so apologetic that they offered me a $200 discount because they could not start on the promised day. When I asked about what day they would resume the job, she said it would be only a week later. I thanked her for her honesty and for the gesture of good will, but I did not need the discount. It was not out of negligence or poor planning that he could not keep on schedule, but rather a medical necessity that postponed the work, and without any coercion he had tried to make the situation better. He took responsibility for his situation plus credited my bill anyway, and that was honorable and a breath of fresh air for me. He and others like him should be commended; the rest should follow their lead.

By taking responsibility for our actions, we take control of our lives and start to eliminate the illusions that we create. One must never forget that we are all connected and affect one another. By taking accountability for our actions in the dojo and in our lives, we make a profound difference for the better. Now is the time to start resolving our own issues and returning to a happier way of life.

道場

Outside the Dojo

Often students will ask if there is anything that they should do at home to better prepare for their Aikido training. What is interesting about this question is that all aspects of life, both in and out of the dojo, can be considered Aikido, and Aikido principles can be applied to all of life. How far a person goes into integrating Aikido into their lives is totally up to them, but the more effort a person puts into incorporating it into their daily lives relates to how significant the results will be.

Shouldn't we always be aware of our surroundings, especially after we have left the dojo? Don't we need to put our focus and spirit into doing everything, including our jobs to the best of our ability? Everything, from the way we view the world to the way we interact with others, can be positively influenced by Aikido. That being said, to become a good martial artist you must practice the martial arts. One does not improve at math by studying literature, and so to excel in Aikido, take the exercises of the dojo home and practice them. However, there are definite complementary activities, not replacements, that can be done to help develop the body and the mind. One must first have the discipline to practice them regularly and consistently in order to see results.

Practice Things Relating to Aikido

Practice makes perfect. This is true of a strike, a throw, or a kata (a pre–arranged set of movements to simulate a combat situation). Every repetition provides a deeper understanding of the movement. An aikido–ka should, therefore, practice even outside of class. For throwing arts like Aikido, one can review falling, rolling, balance drills, and footwork. Unfortunately, it is more difficult for students of the throwing arts to practice their techniques because there is a need for a partner. Sometimes by envisioning the techniques, step by step each day, it helps the mind to integrate the movements into muscle memory. Certain Olympic athletes have used this method before a competition to improve their familiarity with a particular course, track, or routine, resulting in a more successful performance.

Diet

Something that can be done after consulting a nutritionist is making a healthy change in diet. (Most people cringe when I say that.) In order for the body to function at peak efficiency, you must provide it with the best fuel. A person would not put water into a gas tank and expect the car to make it across the country on a long road trip, so why put garbage in your body and expect that you will feel good? The more energy the body has to spend digesting junk food decreases the resources it has to heal and maintain itself. A person cannot achieve the skill of a master if his body is functioning like a novice. The same is true of smoking, drinking alcohol, or using other illicit chemical substances. I never understood how a student or a sensei could work out for an hour or two of class and then go out for a smoke. After training, the body is trying to replenish its oxygen supply in order to return itself to homeostasis. By smoking, you are taking away the thing the body needs and therefore hurting your body. I know quitting smoking is not easy at all, but nothing worth attaining ever is. Stop looking at the short–term "suffering" and do it because it will ultimately improve your quality of life.

If you are unsure about what to eat, speak to a qualified nutritionist or healthcare professional.

Stretching

Stretching is just as important to do after training. I recommend incorporating stretching to help prevent tightness, muscle cramps, and spasms as a way to cool down.

Bodywork

Similarly to stretching, therapeutic bodywork is a great way to help maintain the body, and it also feels good. Modalities like deep tissue massage, Craniosacral therapy, chiropractics, and acupuncture can reduce mental and physical stress, improve muscle tone and fatigue, and increase overall circulation. By getting bodywork as little as once a month, the body will feel better and be less prone to injury during training. People will regularly get oil changes and tune–ups for their car in order to maintain their vehicles, so why not do something to maintain the most important machine we have, our bodies? For those people who feel weird about being touched, just understand that these are simply non–invasive medical procedures that can help to bring the body back into balance. There is nothing sexual about bodywork if done correctly by a properly credentialed practitioner. If disrobing makes you uncomfortable, there are modalities like craniosacral therapy that do not require a client to disrobe. Whatever therapy you choose, first research which modality and therapist suits your needs the best.

Strength Training

Weightlifting can be a good addition to a martial arts routine if done in moderation. Lifting weights can improve muscle strength and increase bone density, which helps the body even in later years. However, when done too often, it can wear down the joints, decrease flexibility, and slow down reaction time due to the bulkiness that can result. Personally, I prefer strength training that can be done at home. Exercises like push–ups, strengthening core abdominal muscles, and resistance training that causes the muscles to work against gravity can be very effective and less expensive than going to a gym. Another option is using therapeutic resistance bands. They are easy to use and cost effective. These also develop long muscle instead of bulk, which is better suited for the martial arts, while at the same time strengthening the connective tissues. Let me reiterate: weightlifting can be beneficial when done in moderation.

Reduce Stress

Stress is defined by the *Merriam–Webster Dictionary* as a physical, chemical, or emotional factor that causes bodily or mental tension and may be a factor in disease causation. Every stress we have impedes the functioning of the body. Therefore, by doing things that reduce stress, we can improve attributes like emotional states and immunity. Hopefully Aikido can be the activity that helps reduce stress for you, although there are many different activities that can reduce stress, depending on the individual. Some include meditation, exercise, playing music, or even enjoying a good meal with a loved one. Whichever activity you choose, make sure that there is time to slow down to enjoy life. Similar to a light bulb that is always on, if we are in a constant state of stress we can eventually burn out.

Exercise the Mind

It would be ridiculous to cultivate the body to peak performance while allowing the mind to deteriorate from inactivity. To have real health and be successful martial artists we must develop the mind as well. The samurai were as skilled with a brush as they were with a sword, and so we too must learn more than combat to be martial artists; otherwise we are just fighters. One thing that can be done to strengthen the mind is reading philosophy. Whether it is on the philosophy of martial arts or "the Tao of Pooh," reading can exercise the mind and open it to reflect on deeper questions. Books on Aikido can further explain the underlying theory on why the art works the way it does. Reading, on the other hand, cannot teach martial arts technique; only regular guidance from a teacher can.

Meditation is another tool that can clear the mind, reduce stress, and help to stabilize emotion. Puzzles and games that challenge the mind are also beneficial. I personally enjoy chess. For children, helping them to use their imagination is also beneficial. By challenging the mind, we grow as martial artists and as people.

Practicing outside the dojo can be just as in–depth as in the dojo if you want it to be. In fact, make Aikido more than just a practice; make it a way of life. Something as simple as walking down the street can be a meditative exercise or a way to develop awareness of our surroundings. Overall, a change in diet, strength training, low impact aerobic exercise and mukuso can provide a healthy and well–rounded routine to compliment your Aikido training.

用語集

Conclusion

It is exciting to me to see how Aikido has evolved from an art of combat, originating from Aikijujutsu, to an art of peace. Ueshiba's conception of the art was revolutionary in his time and still profound in ours. There is something truly unique about Aikido as a form of budo in its application of technique as well as its philosophy as a gentleman's art and an art of tranquility. The transformation that an aikido–ka can go through not only strengthens the body, but restores balance to the spirit. Do not misinterpret the compassionate ideals as weakness in the art, for Aikido when applied correctly, can provide victory in the most difficult of situations. Remember that it is still a method of combat and should be practiced in that way.

As Aikido moves forward, I am sure it will continue to develop. How, nobody knows, but my wish is that as it develops, it is not watered down in order to cater to the masses, but rather adapted into modern times while preserving the traditions, knowledge, and intensity that makes Aikido great. Since Aikido is an ideal art for children, I would also love to see it become a regular part of the physical education curriculum in our public schools.

I hope *Enter into Aikido* has inspired you to pursue this art to its fullest depths because Aikido has inspired me to be who I am today.

Glossary of Terms

Body Parts

ashi—foot

empi—elbow

hiza—knee

hon—finger

kata—shoulder

kubi—neck

shomen—top or front of head

te—hand

tekubi—wrist

te–ashi—ankle

ude/katate—arm

yokomen—side of the head

Stances and Footwork

ai hanmi—half–body stance

ayumi ashi—walking footwork

gyaku–dachi—reverse stance

gyaku hanmi—reverse half–body stance

ippon tai sabaki—one full body pivot

irimi—entering

jigotai/jigotai dachi—defensive stance

jigohantai—forward defensive stance

kibodachi—horse stance

kosadachi—cross stance

nekko ashi dachi—cat foot stance

renoshidachi—fencer's stance

shikkowaza/shinkiwaza—knee walking techniques

shizentaidachi–natural posture

taema tai sabaki—continuous body pivots

tai sabaki—body pivots

tenkan—turn

tsugi ashi—following footwork

wazari tai sabaki—half–body pivot

zenkutsudachi—locked–leg stance

Blocks

age uke—rising block

chuden ude uke—center level arm block

gedan barai uke—downward sweeping block

gedan osae uke—lower pressing block

gedan ude uke—lower level arm block

joden ude uke—upper level arm block

juji–uke—cross block

te uke—hand block

tsuru uke—crane block

ude ki uke—arm internal energy block

Atemi–Strikes

age uchi—rising strike

empi–uchi—elbow strike

geri—kick

mae geri—front snap kick

yoko–geri—side kick

mawashi–geri—roundhouse kick

kansetsu–geri—joint lock kick

ushiro–geri—rear kick

gyaku–tsuki—reverse lunge punch

gyaku–yokomen–uchi—reverse side of head strike

hiza ate—knee strike

kage–tsuki—hook punch

koko–uchi—tiger mouth strike

mawashi–tsuki—round house punch

mune–tsuki—breast strike

oi tsuki—forward lunge punch

riken–uchi—back knuckle strike

sayu–tsuki—double–fist lunge punch

shomen–uchi—head strike

shuto–uchi—knife hand

tate–tsuki—vertical hand lunge punch

te–uchi—hand strike

tegatana–uchi—sword hand

tetsui–uchi—bottom fist strike

tsuki—lunging strike

ue–tsuki—rising vertical punch

ura–tsuki—close in punch

yokomen–uchi—side of head strike

yoko–tetsuiuchi—side bottom fist strike

yonhon–nukite—four–finger thrust

Aikido Terminology

agatsu—self victory

ai—harmony

arigato–Thank you

bo–wooden staff approximately six feet in length

bokken—wooden sword

budo—martial way

bugei/bujutsu–martial art of war

bukiwaza–weapons techniques

dan—black belt rank

do—way or path

dojo–training hall

domo arigato gozaimashita—thank you very much

doshu—the head of a way

dogi/gi—training uniform

dozo–please

hai–yes

hajime–begin

hakama—black baggy pants that look like a skirt and were worn by the samurai and by practitioners of the sword and the throwing arts

hara—center of gravity in our body located about four inches below the navel and considered a storage area of spirit and ki

henkawaza—one technique changing into another mid movement

hombu–headquarters

iaido–way of drawing the sword

iaijutsu–sword drawing art of war

iei–no

irimi—entering movement

jo—four–foot staff

jodo—way of the staff

kaeshiwaza—reversal techniques

kamiza—small shrine usually found in the front of the dojo

kansetsuwaza—joint–locking techniques

katatedori/katatetori—wrist grab hold

kata—a prearranged set of movements that simulate a combat situation

katame/gatame—a pin or hold

katana—samurai sword

ken—sword

ki—internal or universal energy

kiai—a loud shout to startle an opponent while harnessing focus to complete a task

kihon—a basic technique or exercise

ki musubi—literally means "the tying of ki" and means the connection and blending of movement between attacker and defender

kohai—a student junior to oneself

kokyu—breath

koshiita–board on the back of the hakama

kumijo—paired jo practice

kumitachi—paired sword practice

kuzushi—destroying of one's balance

kyu—student rank

ma–ai—proper balance

misogi—ritual cleansing and a way of purifying oneself of negative characteristics

mudansha—student grade

mushin—"no mind"

mae chugeri—front high break fall

mae ukemi—front fall

mae zempo kaiten—front rotary roll

masakatsu agatsu—the true mastery of self victory

nafuda kake—rank board with members names

nagewaza—throwing techniques

newaza/tatamiwaza—ground work techniques

obi—belt

okuden—"entrance to secrets" usually a title for those entering the dan ranks

osaewaza—holding or pinning techniques

o–sensei—great teacher. in aikido morihei ueshiba, the father of aikido, is often called o–sensei

randori—freestyle practice often with multiple attackers

reigi/reishiki—etiquette

seiza—seated position

sempai—senior student

sempei—apprentice

sensei—teacher

shihan—a master level title meaning "one who points the way"

shodan—first degree black belt

shomen—front or top of the head, also the front of a dojo

shukaku– the dead angle

soke–dai—sucessor

soto—outside

suburi—cut

suwariwaza—techniques done with both partners in a seated position

taijutsu—unarmed training

tai sabaki—body pivot

tanto—a type of knife

tenkan—turn

tori/nage—person performing the technique

uchi deshi—live in student

ushiro ukemi—back fall

uke—person receiving the technique

waza–technique

ushiro zempo kaiten—rear rotary roll

yoko ukemi—side fall

yoko chugeri—side high break fall

yudansha—black belt rank

zanshin—a complete focus and awareness of our self and our surroundings

Directions

hidari—left

mae—front

migi—right

omote—"life side" when a practitioner enters in front of or across another while performing technique

ushiro—rear

ura—circle

yoko—side

Aikido Techniques

ikkyo—first principle

nikkyo—second principle

sankyo—third principle

yonkyo—fourth principle

gokyo—fifth principle

jujinage—cross arms throw

kaiten nage—rotary throw

kokyunage—breath throw

koshinage—hip throw

kotegaeshi—wrist twist

shihonage—four directions throw
sayu undo—left and right exercise
tenchinage—heaven and earth throw

Various names of aikido techniques are put together by first naming the attack, then the technique, and finally either a direction or a number to be used as a reminder. An example of this would be the technique Ai hanmi katatedori shihonage omote. Ai hanmi katatedori is the attack, shihonage is the technique, and omote is the direction. Here are some other examples.

Ai hanmi katatedori kokyu nage
Gyaku hanmi katatedori kokyu nage
Yokomen uchi kokyu nage
Ai hanmi katatedori shihonage omote
Ai hanmi katatedori shihonage ura
Gyaku hanmi katatedori shihonage omote
Gyaku hanmi katatedori shihonage ura
Yokomenuchi shihonage omote
Yokomenuchi shihonage ura
Shomenuchi shihonage omote
Shomenuchi shihonage ura
Ai hanmi katatedori kotegaeshi omote
Ai hanmi katatedori kotegaeshi ura
Gyaku hanmi katatedori kotegaeshi omote
Gyaku hanmi katatedori kotegaeshi ura
Munetsuki kotegaeshi omote

Munetsuki kotegaeshi ura

Ai hanmi katatedori ikkyo omote

Ai hanmi katatedori ikkyo ura

Gyaku hanmi katatedori ikkyo omote

Gyaku hanmi katatedori ikkyo ura

Shomenuchi ikkyo omote

Shomenuchi ikkyo ura

Ai hanmi katatedori nikkyo omote

Ai hanmi katatedori nikkyo ura

Gyaku hanmi katatedori nikkyo omote

Gyaku hanmi katatedori nikkyo ura

Ai hanmi katatedori sankyo omote

Ai hanmi katatedori sankyo ura

Gyaku hanmi katatedori Kaiten nage omote

Gyaku hanmi katatedori Kaiten nage ura

Shomenuchi kaiten nage omote

Shomenuchi kaiten nage ura

Riotedori kokyu nage

Riotedori ikkyo

Riotedori nikkyo

Riotedori Sankyo

Riotedori tenchinage omote

Riotedori tenchinage ura

Riotedori shihonage omote

Riotedori shihonage ura

Ushiro riotedori/riokatadori kokyu nage

Ushiro riotedori/riokatadori ikkyo

Ushiro riotedori/riokatadori nikkyo

Ushiro riotedori/riokatadori Sankyo

Ushiro riotedori/riokatadori tenchinage omote

Ushiro riotedori/riokatadori tenchinage ura

Ushiro riotedori/riokatadori shihonage omote

Ushiro riotedori/riokatadori shihonage ura

Ushiro riotedori/riokatadori koshinage

Ushiro riotedori/riokatadori jujinage

Ushiro riotedori/riokatadori tenbinage

Ushiro riotedori/riokatadori sayu undo

List of Foreign Words

soke

sifu

aikido

fukasa–kai/fukasa–ryu/
fukasa–ryu bujutsukai

dojo

ki

aikijutsu

kempo

jujutsu

iaijutsu

kenjutsu

aiki–ken

kendo

iaido

aiki–jodo

tai chi

qigong

judo

kobudo

kobujutsu

soke–dai

tanto–jutsu

bo–jutsu

naginata–jutsu

so–jutsu

muay thai

jeet kune do

kali

escrima

aikido–ka

jujutsu

bujutsu

budo

aiki–budo

daito–ryu aikijujutsu

in & yo
yoseikan
yoshinkan
ki no kenyu–kai
shin shin toitsu
aikikai
iwama–ryu
tomiki–ryu
randori
skinkiwaza
shimewaza
nage–waza
ne–waza
atemi–waza
kyu
dan
kuzushi
karate–do
kata
kumite–waza
shorin–ryu
goju–ryu
koryu
gendai budo
doshu
hakama
obi

gi
ukemi
menkyo
shoden
chuden
joden
okuden
kyoshi
shihan–dai
shihan
soke–dai
shokaku
mudansha
yadansha
kodokan
shodan–ho
shoshin
reishiki
rei
shiki
shomen
kamiza
bushi
omoto–kyo
ritsurei
zarei
seiza

sensei–ni–rei

domo arigato gozaimasu

mokuso

ki–o–tsuke

shimoza

dogi

himo

misogi

hai

tatami

uke

nage

chageri

mae

ushiro

yoko

mae zempo kaiten

ushiro zempo kaiten

koshinage

kama

tonfa/tuifa

sai

nunchaku

kobujutsu

kamae

ai

yagyo–ryu

kashima shinto–ryu

hozoin so–jutsu

hanbo/aiki–hanbo

suburi–to

shinai

kote

kyujutsu/kyudo

o–sensei

goshinjutsu

shodan

nikkyo

saho

kotegaeshi

prana

hara

hanmi

nidan

sandan

Endnotes

1. Legitimate styles are discussed further in the chapter "Legitimacy in the Martial Arts."

2. Ki refers to vital life force or internal energy and is discussed further in the chapter "The Myth and Mystery of Ki."

3. Subjects were divided into a qigong group of 122 patients and a control group of 120 non–practitioners. Both groups took standard hypertensive drugs. Subjects were tracked over a 30–year period of time. At the end of this period, 47.76% of the control group had died. Only 25.41% of the Qigong group died. These are very significant results, with a probability of less than one in 1,000 of being due to chance. The incidence of stroke in the control group being 40.83%, and in the qigong group 20.49%. The incidence of death due to stroke was 32.50% among the controls, in the qigong group, 15.57%. These results are also statistically significant, with less than one chance in 100 (p<0.01).

Bibliography

Books

Westbrook, A and Ratti, O. *Aikido and the Dynamic sphere*. Rutland, Vermont and Tokyo Japan: Charles E. Tuttle Publishing Co. 1970

————. *Secrets of the Samurai: The martial arts of Feudal Japan*. Rutland, Vermont and Tokyo, Japan: Charles E: Tuttle Publishing Co. 1973

Draeger, Donn and Smith, Robert. *Comprehensive Asian Fighting Arts*. Bunkyo–ku, Tokyo: Kodansha International 1969

Dang, Phong Thong and Seiser, Lynn. *Aikido Basics*. North Clarendon, Vermont: Charles E Tuttle Publishing Co. 2003

Tsunemoto, Yamamoto. *Hagakure The book of the Samurai*. Otowa 1–chome, Bunkyo–ku, Tokyo, Japan: Kodansha America, Inc. 1979

Tolle, Eckhart. *The Power of Now : A guide to Spiritual Enlightenment.* Canada: Namaste Publishing Inc. 1997

Bishop, Mark. *Zen Kobudo: Mysteries of Okinawan Weaponry and Te.* Rutland, Vermont and Tokyo, Japan: Charles E: Tuttle Publishing Co. 1996

Suenaka, Roy and Watson, Christopher. *Complete Aikido—Aikido Kyohan: The Definitive Guide to the way of Harmony.* Boston, Massachusetts: Charles E Tuttle Publishing Co. 1997

Ueshiba, Kisshomaru. *The Spirit of Aikido.* Bunkyo–ku, Tokyo: Kodansha International 1988

Internet

"Judoinfo.com." *Neil Ohlenkamp* July 10, 2006 <http://judoinfo.com/whatis.htm>

"aikidofaq.com." <www.aikidofaq.com/misc/hakama.html>

"Aikido Tenshinkai of Florida." <www.Aikitenshi.com>

"Japanese Martial Arts Tradition." S. Banchick 2002–03 <http://www.anotherpath.com/kespresbar/hshoes.html>

"Fukasa Ryu Bujutsukai." Cary Nemeroff July 27th, 2008 <www.fukasakai.com>

"Canadian & International Shito–Ryu Karate Resource Centre." Sam Moledzki 2008 <www.shitoryu.org>

"Judoinfo.com:Mikonosuke Kawaishi: Judo Teacher in Europe." Neil Ohlenkamp April 1, 2007 <www.judoinfo.com/kawaishi.htm>

"World History.com" site no longer available <http://www.worldhistory.com/wiki/H/Hakama.htm>

"Koryu.com:A koryu Primer." Diane Skoss December 29, 2007 <www.koryu.com/koryu.html>

About the Author

David Nemeroff was born and raised in Middletown, New York, by his parents, Bernard and Susan. He had his initial exposure to the martial arts there at the age of seven after taking a karate class at a local community college. He became more serious about his training after being introduced to the art of aikido at the age of twelve under the tutelage of Robert MacEwen Jr., Sensei. As a teenager he added to his training and began studying with Cary Nemeroff, Soke, who is still one of his teachers to this day. Around the age of twenty, he was introduced to his current Aikido teacher, Dr. Jose Andrade, Sensei and became accepted as a member of Kokusai Budoin, Tokyo, Japan soon after.

Since that time, he has trained continuously to improve his knowledge and skills, earning black belts in several different martial arts, including three different aikido systems: aikijutsu, Kempo, jujutsu, aiki–jodo (way of the four–foot staff), Aiki–hanbo (three foot staff), Iaijutsu, and Kenjutsu (samurai sword). In addition, he has supplemented his training with such arts as Tai Chi, Qigong, judo, Kobudo, Tanto–jutsu, Bo–jutsu, Naginata–jutsu and So–jutsu, Muay thai, Jeet kune do, Kali, and Escrima.

Mr. Nemeroff is certified from both Japan and the United States and has more than twenty–three years of martial arts experience. Recently, he was awarded the title of *Soke–Dai* (Successor) to Fukasa–Ryu Aikido and is the division head for this particular style of aikido. In 1999 he was also certified as a lethal weapons training instructor under Act 235 by the Pennsylvania State Police.

He has taught martial arts to several groups, including corporations like Mack Truck, Air Products, Guardian Life Insurance, and Agere, students at Penn State University, Kid's Peace, Boys and Girls Club, army reserve units, police officers, and security guards. Additionally, he has been published in *Aikido Today Magazine* as well as local publications. Mr. Nemeroff attained a B.S. in fine arts/graphic design from Hofstra University and is a national board–certified massage therapist specializing in craniosacral therapy.

It is the culmination of these experiences that allow him to bring a wealth of knowledge, as well as honesty, humility, and honor, to the martial arts.